KV-141-277

Contents

	Authors and Contributors	vii
	Acknowledgements	ix
1	Introduction and Case Histories	1
2	Historical and Social Considerations	20
3	Families and Handicap	32
4	Assessment	44
5	The Role of the Physiotherapist, Occupational Therapist and Speech Therapist	57
6	Education	65
7	Work, Employment and Training	78
8	Recreation and Leisure Opportunities	90
9	Residential Needs	99
10	Life in an Institution and Beyond	112
11	Sexuality and Personal Relationships	123
12	Staffing Issues	137
13	Causes and Prevention of Secondary Disabilities and Handicaps	152
14	Difficult and Inappropriate Behaviour	162
15	When People with a Mental Handicap Grow Old	179
16	Biomedical Causation	195
17	Commonly Associated Disorders: Epilepsy and Cerebral Palsy	211
	Epilogue: Future Changes	234

Bibliography	239
Useful Addresses	240
Index	243

Authors and Contributors

John Hattersley BSc, MSc, ABPsS
Top Grade Clinical Psychologist
Mental Handicap Services Unit
Sheffield Health Authority

Gwilym Hosking MB, BS, MRCP, DCH
Consultant Paediatric Neurologist
Ryegate Children's Centre *and* the Children's
   Hospital, Sheffield

David Morrow RMN, RNMH
Director of Nursing Services
Mental Handicap Services Unit
Sheffield Health Authority

Mary Myers MRCS, LRCP, FRCPsych, DPM
Consultant Psychiatrist in Mental Handicap
Mental Handicap Services Unit
Sheffield Health Authority

Contributors for Chapter 5:

S. R. Bell MCSP
Superintendent Physiotherapist
Mental Handicap Services, Sheffield

H. Berry LCST
Chief Speech Therapist
Mental Handicap Services, Sheffield

S. M. Hubbard DipCOT
Head Occupational Therapist
Mental Handicap Services, Sheffield

Acknowledgements

The authors thank Steven Bell, Hilary Berry and Sue Hubbard for contributing Chapter 5.

They also thank Elaine Benton, Lynn Fisher and Beverley Turner for typing and retyping the chapters. They thank particularly Beverley Turner who has organised much of the co-ordination of the authors.

Note on use of terminology

It will be noted that in this book a variety of terms have been
employed in relation to 'people with a mental handicap'. The
variation in terminology exists between the authors and even
within contributions made by each author. For this the authors
make no apology as it is their feeling that the varying use of terminology does reflect on aspects of changing perspectives on
intellectual disability. The authors believe that whatever terminology is employed by them or others the crucial issue is that first
and foremost it is people to whom they are referring.

Note on use of case studies

The authors wish to emphasise that the case studies described are
purely fictional and bear no known relation to actual persons.

Chapter 1

Introduction and Case Histories

This book has been written for those people who serve or support individuals who have severe learning difficulties. We hope it will help parents, teachers, therapists, nurses and many other professionals who are involved regularly or at intervals in the lives of people who have a mental handicap.

Readers will notice that we refer to *people* with a disability or handicap. We are emphasising that men, women and children are people first and 'handicapped' second. The book is based on the recognition that all people grow, change and develop throughout life and that the opportunities and experiences at each stage are affected by past events and will in turn affect future developments. We are all conscious of how little interest has been paid in the past to the life events of many adults who have a mental handicap. Their emotional experiences of success, failure, loss, achievement, love, have been held of little account. At the end of this chapter there are short stories about four people and some of the problems that they and their families experience. The causes of some of their difficulties will, we hope, become clearer in subsequent chapters and, with a change in attitude and style of service, may instead enrich and empower people's lives. Some of our suggestions may be novel and even challenging to some readers, but in parts of North America the new approaches have been applied and refined for nearly 15 years. We are grateful to our transatlantic colleagues for demonstrating to us ways ahead and what mistakes we must avoid. It is a pity that service providers in the United Kingdom (UK) have so little interest in the achievements and lessons of elsewhere, and so often continue to re-invent square wheels. We might ask, who in fact are the slow learners?

There is a question of terminology. 'Mental handicap' has had a variety of names: mental deficiency, mental defect, mental retardation, mental subnormality (Mental Health Act 1959) are all British terms. The Mental Health Act, 1983 introduced the regrettable term 'mental impairment' to identify the condition of individuals who, in addition to having intellectual difficulties, are limited in their social functioning and also present seriously anti-social behaviour. 'Mental impairment' is a vague, meaningless term better applied when someone is drunk or drugged. It is an inaccurate and unhelpful term which will not be referred to in this book except in a brief mention of the Mental Health Act, 1983. Whatever term is chosen, we are concerned about people of any age who from early in life have severe learning difficulties. The nature of the difficulties will vary and the effect they have on how the individual lives will vary too, but the underlying problem is primarily an educational one. How do we enable an individual to continue learning to become self-determining, to develop good relationships, and have a good image of himself?

In analysing and then addressing the mixed problems of people with handicaps it is very useful to apply the World Health Organisation's 'Classification of Impairment Disability and Handicap' (1980). Put briefly the Classification states that:

Impairment is any *loss* or abnormality of psychological, physiological or anatomical *structure or function*.

Disability is any *resulting* restriction or *lack of ability to perform* an activity considered normal.

Handicap is a *disadvantage* resulting from impairment or disability, which restricts or *prevents the fulfilment of a role* that is normal (for the age, sex and culture).

Some common examples will illustrate the terms (Table 1).

Table 1   To illustrate the classification of terms relative to handicap

Impairment	Disabilities	Handicaps
Eye injury →	Blindness	→ Loss of orientation and communication Loss of learning At risk of environmental hazards
Brain damage →	Cerebral palsy (movement and speech) Learning difficulties Epilepsy	→ Segregation Low expectations Loss of opportunities to explore and play Unable to make speech sounds
Extra chromosome 21 →	Common physical problems of Down's syndrome (e.g. short sight, infections, deafness, heart defects) Intellectual disability	→ Segregation Low expectations Loss of opportunities and learning Incompetence Low self-image

Although it is usually, but not totally, impossible to restore an *impairment*, technology of all kinds now makes it possible to reduce *disability*, and a combination of technology and social attitudes can reduce and avoid *handicaps*.

Using these definitions it perhaps becomes apparent why 'intellectual disability' is a more appropriate term than 'mental handicap' for the problem experienced by people with severe learning difficulties. 'Intellectual' is a more accurate description than 'mental', which is a term associated with psychiatry rather than learning; 'disability' directs attention to the need *to enable* the person by whatever means are possible, recognising that impaired movement, vision, hearing and speech commonly compound the learning difficulties further.

In Chapter 2 it is shown how people with severe learning difficulties and associated problems have been recognised by their communities throughout history and why so many individuals came to be gathered in asylums and hospitals. A number of people in asylums had an identifiable biological impairment to learning, that is, they had a medical condition which affected their development or functioning, and professional responsibility for their care was left to the medical profession, in particular, psychiatrists. With the advent of the National Health Service, the lives of thousands of people with severe learning difficulties became the responsibility of health professionals instead of educationalists. In Britain since 1970 changes have been occurring. There has been a great effort to prevent the biological impairment from occurring at all, and that is the responsibility of obstetricians, paediatricians, and health educationists. In addition, the management of children who are impaired is now shared by child health professionals and teachers, with education having the major responsibility throughout childhood and adolescence. As an individual outgrows the need for services to children, however, his/her continuing need for planned help with learning adult roles and responsibilities seems to be ignored. The problems are still seen to be the responsibility of Health and Social Services Departments, which struggle to find answers to the wrong questions. Some ways forward which we consider to be essential for adults with severe learning difficulties will be suggested in subsequent chapters.

The term 'care in the community' has now become a threadbare cliché and, like all generalisations, has been interpreted in many ways, usually very loosely. Since the 1970s, there have been continuing changes in attitude in Britain about the rights and needs of people who are intellectually disabled, but they have started from a paternalistic view developed about society's responsibilities to such individuals; whereas in North America the emphasis has been on the civil rights of people with developmental disabilities to be supported in the least restrictive environment, and that means in their own (and not necessarily the parents') home. Recognising the full human rights of people with disability means that they do not have to prove themselves '*capable* of living in the community' to somebody else's satisfaction, before being allowed out of the residential unit. That is, they do not have to meet the service's criteria: instead the service must meet their needs.

This fundamental conceptual turnabout has not been grasped by many health authority and social services departments. It turns many practices on their heads and challenges the status of service providers. Several small local initiatives were started in Britain for children with a mental handicap, placing them in twos and threes in ordinary houses with their own staff during the late 1970s. These were followed with similar pilot schemes for adults, and knowledge of their success, as shown by leaps in personal development of the residents, became widespread. To run a big institution is very expensive; some 30 per cent of the costs go on fabric, the grounds, and heating high ceilings and draughty corridors. Money saved from such areas when residents are resettled in ordinary houses can be used to employ more human help. The Department of Health and Social Security (DHSS) has promoted the concept of providing 'care in the community' and at one stage suggested that it might be cheaper than institutional care. Practitioners rapidly dismissed that notion, pointing out that chronically under-funded services, already grossly inadequate in the institutions, would never miraculously become better, much cheaper, somewhere else. Nevertheless the means now exist whereby the money spent on a hospital resident can be transferred to provide his or her services in the community. That amount is currently around £12 000 per annum in England and Wales for an adult.

At the present time (1986), service providers and planners are struggling with conflicting demands, and parents are increasingly anxious. There are muddled, ill-understood moves towards 'community care' for hospital residents, but uncertainty about who is eligible (there is a vague judgement that some individuals are not eligible, but the basis of that judgement is insecure). Hospitals are facing closure, but with great delays in defining and designing the alternative comprehensive community services. Only a quarter of UK citizens with severe intellectual disability live in hospitals and can bring their 'dowry' with them to a community service. The other three-quarters have always lived in the community, dependent on parents, and have no 'dowries' to fund their part of the comprehensive service.

There is no doubt that the major changes needed in services to people with intellectual disability will take years to achieve and require more resources. It is essential in our view that their needs are recognised to vary over a lifetime, are properly understood, and that service components are freed from bureaucratic assumptions about the nature of 'mental handicap'.

This book is a contribution to the management of those changes.

CASE STUDIES

Here are the unfinished stories of four people who each has a mental handicap. Some of the themes in their lives will be described in the chapters of this book.

Anne

Anne is 37, single and unemployed. She lives with her widowed mother of 77 who in the past months since a fall has become increasingly forgetful, muddled and irritable. Anne's father died 5 years ago: her married sister Pat, aged 49, lives in the same town and shares her home with her divorced daughter Janet and small grandson.

When Anne was born the doctor informed her father that she

was 'a mongol', and left him to tell his wife. Her parents went through much grief over her condition: Anne was a frail baby and often seriously ill. Her brother and sister were bewildered by their parents' distress and endured much teasing at school about their sister's condition. No advice was available about how to help a little girl with Down's syndrome; her parents were warned that 'she would only ever have the mental age of a child of 7'; unfortunately they treated her for ever after as a younger child.

The school system refused to admit Anne at the age of 5 but she started at a Junior Training Centre where she remained until she was 16, not acquiring any really useful skills. Anne's parents did everything for her and considered her a perpetual child. Anne started at the Adult Training Centre (ATC) at 16 and enjoyed the company of older people. She tried hard to join in adult activities, but her mother would not allow Anne to encounter any risks; for example, she was not allowed to handle hot kettles or go to the corner shop alone. Although her parents feared that one day she might be sexually exploited, they never actually discussed sexual behaviour with her. Anne became friendly with a lad at the ATC and when, one day, they were found exploring one another there was an uproar, and Anne was kept away from the Centre for good.

Anne's brother and sister both married and had children but Anne understood that her role was to stay at home to keep her mum company. She was under-occupied and remained always at her parents' side, being much indulged by them, sometimes with some exasperation. Generally her social life was among her parents' friends, most of whom were involved in the world of mental handicap. One day her father became ill, was taken to hospital and never returned. Anne never knew where he went after that; her mum said he had gone to heaven and she cried a lot. Anne had loved her dad and was puzzled, a bit angry and miserable following his disappearance.

Now her mother is not well, and Anne is worried that her mother might go away and likewise never return. She is scared what will happen to herself then. Anne constantly checks on the whereabouts of her mother, who is exasperated, but at the same time worried about Anne's future when she herself has gone.

Pat is wearied and worried by the deteriorating condition of both her mother and her sister. She recognises how unnecessarily incompetent and inexperienced in all areas of self-care and living Anne has remained, and how dowdy and lacking in self-esteem she is. Pat does not know whether Anne's recent childish demanding behaviour is due to the premature ageing of people with Down's syndrome or because she is emotionally unsettled by her mother's frailty. Their mother is unlikely to live much longer. Pat has not room to give Anne a home but Anne could inherit her mother's house herself if she could be supported to live in it. The local authority dismisses such a suggestion as quite 'unrealistic'. It has also said it has no vacancies in the local hostel, and in any case does not have enough staff to look after people as dependent as Anne.

The three women are increasingly tense and anxious about their futures and the mental health of each of them is deteriorating. Pat is also angry that even 37 years has not been sufficient time for the local authority to plan for her sister's future; she wonders just how long does the authority need?

Peter

Peter is the second child in the family and at the age of 6 years he is clearly severely multiply handicapped with cerebral palsy, severe learning difficulties, poor vision and epilepsy.

Peter's parents are in their late twenties and his older sister is 10. His father is an industrial worker on irregular shifts and in recent years has had periods of working short time. His mother previously had a job as an assistant in a works' canteen but now has an office cleaning job three evenings each week. They live in a small council house situated at the top of a hill. It has three bedrooms and a very small garden. They have a small car, but it is old and often subject to breakdown. It needs replacing but at the present this does not seem feasible because of a shortage of money.

Both parents come from the area in which they live. The maternal grandmother is a frequent visitor to the home and provides much support. The paternal grandmother seldom visits: she has a husband with severe Parkinson's disease who needs a lot of help; but besides that she is not fond of her daughter-in-law, and never has been.

Peter was a much wanted baby and his parents were delighted when the pregnancy was confirmed, as they had been waiting for some time. The pregnancy was reasonably satisfactory. Antenatal classes were attended even though it was difficult for Peter's mother always to get the time off to do so. When she remembered she did take iron and vitamin tables, but continued to smoke about 10 cigarettes a day. She always felt a little guilty about the cigarettes but her attempts to stop them were never completely successful.

One evening when Peter's mother was 7 months' pregnant she started having severe pains which seemed like the onset of labour. She was at a wedding party at the time and was enjoying herself and drinking rather more alcohol than was usual for her. She was admitted to hospital in early labour. Attempts were made to stop the labour but it continued. At this stage it was realised that not only was she in premature labour (8 weeks early) but that the baby was a breech (i.e. coming bottom first).

Labour was rapid and forceps were necessary. Peter weighed only 4½ lb which was small even for a baby who was 8 weeks early. He was very flat and floppy at the time of birth, needing help to start breathing. He was placed in an incubator and immediately transferred to the hospital's special care baby unit. He was not taken to the nursery with the other babies. His mother had an opportunity to see him briefly before he was transferred. The doctor spoke to Peter's father but not to his mother and said it was possible that he might not survive.

It was not until the next day that Peter was seen by his parents. He was in an incubator and had lots of 'tubes and wires' attached to him and, because he was not able to breathe by himself, was on a ventilator. Again the doctors explained that Peter was very ill and would need a lot of help if he was going to survive. At that stage nobody mentioned that he could be handicapped if he did survive.

On the second day of life he started having fits. For a little while these were treated successfully with an anticonvulsant medicine. On the third day the senior doctor saw both the parents, and for the first time mentioned that if Peter did survive there was a strong chance that he would be handicapped.

That evening Peter's parents found themselves in a very distressed state of mind as they talked over the situation that now confronted them. Their 4-year-old daughter was also upset that her baby brother was ill.

After taking Peter home at 6 weeks it was only a short time before the parents realised that he was quite different from their daughter at the same age. He was extremely difficult to feed. Often when handled he would arch his back and almost shoot out of his parents arms.

Before long both parents found themselves physically and emotionally exhausted. At 4 months Peter developed mild gastro-enteritis. The children's doctor involved with his care at this time saw both parents and said there was little doubt that Peter had a severe form of cerebral palsy which could have been related to the fact that he was born prematurely, but not necessarily so. There were no definite explanations as to why he was going to be significantly handicapped. The parents asked whether it was likely that he would also be mentally retarded. The doctors were evasive on that but said that it had to be a distinct possibility.

Over the ensuing months Peter made very slow progress. There was not even a flicker of a smile until he was over 9 months and even then there was some doubt about it. Feeding did become a little easier as time went by but Peter's sleep pattern was still difficult and he remained very irritable. He was not beginning to sit and had very little mobility.

At a year Peter was seen at a child development centre. Over several days physiotherapists, speech therapists, occupational therapists, psychologists and children's doctors spent time with him. The diagnosis of cerebral palsy was confirmed and the particular variety was described as 'quadriplegia' which meant that all Peter's limbs were affected, although the left side was worse than the right. Additionally Peter's vision was extremely poor.

A programme was agreed which meant Peter being seen four times a week at the child development centre, which was at the opposite end of town. Public transport would be virtually impossible; father needed the family car for his work, and Peter's mother was unable to drive. Ambulance transport was arranged, but this meant that Peter had to be ready to leave the home at 8.30 a.m. although the ambulance often did not arrive until 10.30. The journey home was similarly somewhat erratic and time-consuming.

Meanwhile family finances were in a poor state. Stress within the family was considerable, and Peter's sister was showing her distress by her demanding behaviour.

At the age of 2½ Peter was given a place in a special nursery for handicapped children. This gave his mother some respite during the day but because of persisting transport difficulties, that respite was very short.

The social worker from the child development centre told Peter's parents about the Attendance Allowance that could be claimed because he was handicapped. In order to get this allowance, however, there had to be a visit to the home by a doctor whom they had not met before. When he did attend he seemed to know very little about Peter and was most uncommunicative when asked questions. Ultimately an Attendance Allowance was given but not at the rate that was anticipated. An appeal was lodged which necessitated another visit by a different doctor. Peter's mother felt somewhat intimidated by these visits and was left with a very firm impression that she was seeking charitable support. This she found hurtful.

The maternal grandmother was most supportive but on several occasions tried to persuade the parents to seek outside medical and other treatments. As the parents had faith in the child development centre, this suggestion unsettled them.

At the age of 4 Peter was considered for a special school. The parents visited and were alarmed to see handicapped children in the school whom they thought were far more disabled than their son, and they worried whether this would hold him back. Peter himself had very little in the way of physical development. He was still not able to sit without support, he could only half roll, he was unable to feed himself and had frequent epileptic fits. There was no sign of any language development.

Six months later (aged 4½) Peter did start at the special school. He was collected each morning by the special transport and brought back: the difficulties of meeting him still persisted.

Finding baby-sitters for Peter was virtually impossible as people were afraid of his fits. Even his maternal grandmother was reluctant to offer this service. The parents therefore never went out or had any meaningful social life.

When Peter started school his parents were delighted as each small advance was made. He was able to chew his food better which made life much easier, and mobility did increase a little. Now that Peter has reached the age of 6 his parents have perhaps fully realised the enormity of his handicap. They have just been seen by their new general practitioner who was asked to call because Peter was unwell. He diagnosed measles. The visit was brief – he seemed to be very busy – but it was his parting comment that had a major impact upon the parents. He said that it was quite clear that Peter was 'grossly mentally and physically handicapped', in short he was 'a cabbage' and 'the best place for him would be in an institution'.

Six weeks ago Peter's mother herself visited the doctor who diagnosed a severe depressive illness and gave her tablets; only three weeks after this Peter's father came home and announced that he had obtained a job with good money, but it would mean his working away from home for at least several months.

Pauline

Pauline is nearly 17; 17 years that have been difficult for both her and her parents. Her birth was fairly normal although a little difficult, but there had been no cause for concern. Her parents, Margaret and Peter, were looking forward to her arrival. They had only just moved into their own house and although finances were stretched, they managed quite well.

Pauline came into the world bright and bouncy but not crying. Her parents had always thought that babies cried when they were born, but having been reassured that was not the case, tried to forget about it. The family were pleased with Pauline's progress in her first year. She was seen regularly at the clinic and although Margaret complained about difficulties with feeding and being kept awake at night, she was again re-assured when told that many babies behaved in this way.

Margaret took a part-time job when Pauline was 1, even though everyone said she shouldn't, and Pauline was taken to a day nursery. Margaret became aware that Pauline did not play like other children, although she couldn't explain what she meant to her husband when they discussed it. Margaret felt unsure and uncomfortable, but was told not to worry by her mother and Peter's mother. The family suggested that things might improve if she stayed at home, but Margaret liked her job and was unwilling to give it up, although she felt guilty about Pauline.

The nursery staff were beginning to point out that Pauline was not concentrating well and was generally disrupting things, particularly the afternoon nap at the nursery. Pauline's behaviour deteriorated and she began running away in the street and kicking people – a very angry child. By the age of 4 Pauline was still not talking very much and always seemed vague to

Margaret. The usual response from people when she expressed concern was, 'she appears a little slow, but no doubt she will catch up when she gets to school'.

Pauline seemed happy to be left on her first morning at school, but within two hours Margaret had been summoned back to school to collect her. Pauline had been very aggressive towards the other children and although she was calmer by the time Margaret arrived, she still seemed anxious. The incident was put down to first-day nerves. The school was not prepared to accept second-day nerves. Pauline had nearly wrecked the classroom and even kicked a teacher. She was taken to the local GP but no real problems could be identified. Pauline went back to school and with lots of perseverance she settled reasonably well. Her work was not of the highest standard and all she wanted to do was to play on the rocking horse, which eventually had to be removed. Everyone in the family felt that something must have happened at the nursery to upset Pauline that was still worrying her. Margaret felt sure that was not the right explanation; she still felt guilty.

Soon after her sixth birthday Pauline's behaviour started to deteriorate again. This meant exclusion from school and intervention by staff from both the education department and the NHS. The education department would not have Pauline back until something was done – but what? The family GP suggested that Pauline should be taken to a child psychiatrist. The earth opened up. How could Margaret tell anyone that – including her husband and parents? When the family heard the news there were lots of suggestions being made but very few of them seemed sensible, and some were quite punitive.

Pauline was eventually taken to see a child psychiatrist who asked a lot of questions, some of which seemed irrelevant, and another appointment was made. Things at home became much worse. Being at home all day with Pauline was terrible. Pauline began to demand attention and if she didn't get it she would shout and scream. It was so bad that Margaret was unable to take her out, and keeping her in became more and more difficult. Pauline would hide keys, put things down the toilet and sometimes hit other children. At the end of two weeks Margaret was feeling homicidal. Her husband seemed indifferent and said she should be able to cope and to pull herself together – but he always seemed keen to get out of the house. Pauline was dominating their lives to an unbelievable degree.

The next visit to the psychiatrist was the last straw. Having only just come to terms with having to see a psychiatrist, they were now told that Pauline was subnormal. The news was devastating. Could she be cured? Was there any treatment? The short answer was no. The only consolation was that her handicap was not severe, and there was some degree of optimism for the future. They went home feeling angry, wondering who was to blame and why it had happened to them. When they told people the news someone suggested that Pauline would be best put away with others like her – but how could they put away a 6-year-old.

Of course, they were given plenty of reasons for doing just that. She would be happier, she would be with others like herself, she could be treated in hospital – 'they' knew what to do with children like that. Feeling overwhelmed by all the arguments, Margaret agreed, although she didn't know why. Margaret and Peter took Pauline to the children's ward of the local mental handicap hospital. Margaret could not believe the number of children that were there, many of them more handicapped than Pauline, and she decided there and then that she would not allow Pauline to be left there.

On looking back Margaret felt it was the visit to the hospital ward that had helped her to come to terms with the situation at home. Pauline started to attend a special school and Margaret found great support from other parents facing similar problems, and staff members were also helpful. Parents arranged regular meetings where Margaret began to see that many parents had a difficult life with similar problems, not only with their handicapped child, but with their family and society at large. Through talking with parents of older children Margaret began to have some idea of future problems, but also benefited from their experiences.

One of the major problems she would have to face was that Pauline looked like a normal child. Other parents had told her that if children or adults looked different people would usually make allowances and show some degree of insight. However, people with a mental handicap who looked ordinary but did not behave as one would expect did not receive the same amount of tolerance. People in the street would blame the adult with them if the person with a mental handicap was seen to be playing up, whereas a child that looked handicapped might be patronised, but never really ignored.

By the time Pauline reached the age of 12 her family had learned to cope, although they still found it difficult when Pauline had tantrums, hid things from them or ran away, and her inability to handle money caused them some distress. The school had done well with her, however, and she could write her name, hold limited conversations and do many household tasks.

Pauline was maturing physically and that began to cause concern. Her parents hardly ever let her out on her own. When Pauline was 15 the school expressed concern that she was 'interfering with other children' and were worried that she might be 'taken advantage of'.

Pauline will be 17 next week. Margaret and Peter feel they have done well with her, although they view the future with concern. The school have told them they will keep Pauline until she is 19, if she behaves – but what then? Home every day – all day? Who could cope with that? 'She won't leave home to marry, we'll have to keep her at home all the time – she won't get a job – we need some help.'

Stephen

Stephen is almost 17 and lives at home with his parents, his older sister Diane who is just about to go to university and his younger brother Mark. Mark is studying for 'O' levels and is finding it extremely difficult as he shares a bedroom with Stephen. Alan, Stephen's father, had joined the army when he was 18, reaching the rank of captain. When he left the army he tried one or two jobs in industrial management and eventually set up his own business making plastic bags. The business was reasonably successful and the family now lived in a three-bedroomed detached house in a small village. His work demanded a lot of Alan and he regularly worked late. As the firm expanded he was often away at weekends. His wife, Mary, used to teach before the children were born. Moving around the country when Alan was posted meant she had never quite settled down to having a full-time career. She sometimes wished she could go back to work, but Stephen had taken up so much of her time that she now felt out of touch and had lost confidence in her own abilities.

Stephen was attending a local special school. Stephen's school had been very supportive, particularly to his mother. She had regularly attended the parent group and had helped to run the toy library based at the school. Stephen was less able than many of the children in his class, and had gradually become quite demanding in the last two years. He was occasionally aggressive, particularly if he didn't get his own way or if someone wanted him to do something that he did not want to do. He was quite tall, rather overweight and very strong. This added to his stubborn streak and made him extremely difficult to deal with. His father was very strict and rarely had any problems with Stephen. This made the situation worse because he did not understand why his wife and the school had problems.

Stephen had developed a number of behaviours which were very disruptive. He would destroy things around the house, pulling knobs off the TV set, or throwing things down the drain. In his earlier years he had been labelled as slightly autistic. As he had grown up he had developed a communication problem, and people found it difficult to understand him. This often led to his becoming frustrated, particularly when people pretended they understood, and yet failed to meet his demands. More recently, the affection he had learned to show to people had become less appropriate as he had become more sexually aware. His size and his strength meant that some people were becoming afraid of him and embarrassed by his behaviour. His mother and father were uncertain how to deal with his growing sexual awareness, and although they had tried to insist that he went to his bedroom whenever he attempted to masturbate, the fact that he shared a bedroom made this impractical. His older sister had stopped bringing her friends to the house and she was now desperate to get away from home in order to leave the problem behind.

His local school had recently reviewed Stephen's progress and were suggesting that he might have to move school in order that he could carry on receiving education until he was 19. They felt that he was a bad influence on other pupils at the school and that he would be better catered for at the local hospital school. His parents had visited the hospital school and were concerned that Stephen might be a danger to the very severely handicapped pupils. A change in school would also mean that he would have to travel 15 miles each way, by taxi, and that it would be hard for his mother to maintain a regular contact with the school. At the recent review held by the school there was some discussion about Stephen's future. Apparently the only possible occupation for him would be at an ATC and it was becoming more and more difficult to find places. They did talk about the possibility of some form of sheltered employment for Stephen but his communication problem and his challenging behaviour made it unlikely that he would be accepted for such a job.

Stephen had been receiving an occasional visit from a community nurse who had recently arranged for him to be seen by a psychiatrist. There was some discussion about his sexual problems and the possibility of giving him some medication to control them was discussed. Alan and Mary were not keen on this, but were also unable to accept that Stephen would need some sort of sex education. They had left this to the school with their non-handicapped children and felt that it was again up to the school to sort this out with Stephen. They had received advice in the past on dealing with Stephen's behaviour problems, but much of the advice seemed to imply that they were at least partly to blame. Each time the psychologist had made suggestions it seemed that they were expected to change what *they* did with Stephen. They had failed to agree on a different way of handling him, particulary as Alan did not seem to have the same problems. Mary could not be strict in the way that Alan was, and gradually came to feel more and more guilty that it was her fault that Stephen was so disruptive. This was made worse by the fact that until recently the school had always said that he was not a problem. It had been quite a shock but a great relief when the psychologist described some of the difficulties school had also experienced.

It was hard to contemplate the future when there was so much uncertainty about the present. Stephen and his behaviour seemed to seek out all the weak spots both in individuals and in the family as a whole. If he was to progress to have a happy life both he and his family would need a great deal of sensitive and flexible support.

Chapter 2

Historical and Social Considerations

Some of the most important factors leading to any individual's being labelled as 'different' are social. The range of people making up any population has always included some who are more able than the average as well as those who are less able. The end result of being less able or having some impairment has changed as the needs, beliefs, expectations, values and social conscience of any group of people have changed. In particular the use of particular labels by groups of people to describe intellectually impaired individuals is dependent on different features in different societies. In turn, the way each society deals with people so labelled will be different and likely to change over time. How mental handicap is defined in Britain, for example, has changed considerably throughout history and the labels in use have changed over time.

Human beings have a long history of joining together in groups to gather food, to hunt and to provide themselves with defence. Over thousands of years of evolution there was a change from a nomadic life to a more settled existence, based around agriculture. During the nomadic period most severely impaired children probably died at birth. Others who survived, but who showed obvious physical problems which would prevent them from becoming hunters or keeping up with the group, were probably victims of infanticide. The survival of the group as a whole would have been threatened if they had been allowed to live. It is likely, however, that many of the people who today would be labelled mildly intellectually handicapped were able to contribute usefully to their simple society, thus avoiding their own extinction. The gradual change to a more settled life on the land almost certainly made it easier for people with a mental handicap to be integrated into communities.

As society became more industrial, and the demands for a controlled and structured workforce grew, the impact on families and their less able members must have been dramatic. Anyone in a family who was able was required to earn a living by working in the factories. Such factories, with the pressure to make a profit through quick and efficient production, were no place for anyone with physical or mental impairments. The place for such a person in the home or the village also became usurped. Families often moved into towns to be near work and were no longer able to find simple but productive tasks for their less able members. This led to family members who were non-productive either being locked up at home or turned out on to the streets to fend for themselves. As in the earlier nomadic societies there was no room for the individual who was unable to contribute or who became a drain on the resources of the family or society.

In the nineteenth century there was a growing interest in the education of the masses. Through education the workforce could be improved both as 'raw material' for the workplace and in terms of their social behaviour. At the same time there was some evidence that even the most severely impaired might benefit from education. The apparent 'animal nature' of such individuals was still not questioned, but education was seen to be the mechanism for ameliorating such a state. The intention of the reformers of the time was to provide education in schools and asylums in order to transform the solitary, pointless lives of such impaired individuals into something which was worth while, social and industrious. Reports of the work of such asylums and schools portrayed them as places where patience and firmness, without physical coercion or any form of brutality, were used by teachers to gain authority over children. Good physical health, obtained through exercise, nutritious food and hygiene, was seen as the key to improving mental health. The apparent need for people with a mental handicap to be with others with similar problems was deduced from the observations that children with a mental impairment were often isolated from other 'normal' children when they lived at home. The plan, based on sincere beliefs, was to use the protective environment of the asylum to habilitate individuals, through education and good physical care, to become useful and acceptable members of society. Even though it was accepted that there were some individuals who could never benefit, and who would require extensive care and support throughout their lives, the asylums and schools still failed to achieve their stated goal of returning people to a useful life. There were, no doubt, many reasons for this failure, including the very nature of the society into which people were expected to fit and the over-optimistic ideals of the reformers and educators. The most immediately available source of blame for the failures, however, was the victims themselves. The natural conclusion was that people with a mental handicap were at fault and could not be expected to appreciate anything but a life of custody and segregation.

The total institutions thus created were also available to meet other social needs. The government of the time was faced with an increasing number of people, including the poor, invalids, illegitimate children, and the mentally ill, who threatened the very structure of the new, industrial, town-based society. Many institutions began to specialise and to cater for particular groups. The result was an expansion both in the number of people labelled as 'idiots' and in the criteria or reasons used to give such a label.

CAUSES

The way each society responded to people with a mental handicap was also determined in part by the beliefs that existed about the causes of their problems. The many causes which have been proposed contain a mixture of religious, hereditary and environmental factors.

In some of the earliest cultures diseases and mental disorders were attributed to the person's being possessed by devils or being punished by God for some sin committed by themselves or their parents. Many sins were postulated including such things as touching someone who was sick or treading in polluted water. This provided a multitude of potential causes. The great teachers and prophets of history had a major impact on these views. The teachings of Jesus, for example, provided a basis both for a belief that the mentally impaired were possessed by the devil as well as for the practice of caring for society's weakest members. Much of the guilt carried by families, particularly mothers, in our modern culture can probably be traced to such beliefs, especially as there are still many children born with a mental impairment for which no clear cause can be established.

Through the Middle Ages the majority of people in society worked hard, for long hours, usually on the land, in an effort to survive in a hostile world. Their lives and families were regularly destroyed by plagues, natural disasters and wars. As a result superstition, belief in the devil and belief in all-powerful Gods, led to the use of a wide range of practices designed to protect them or to ease their difficulties.

During the Middle Ages the Catholic Church gradually changed its attitude towards mentally impaired people and, with the doctrine of original sin, they became transformed from children of God and Holy Innocents into the creations of the devil or changelings. The Inquisition also led to some people with mental handicap being tortured and executed as witches and wizards. It was during the reign of King Edward II, that the Law recognised (for the well off) the need to safeguard the property of 'natural fools' during their lifetime by taking custody of it. On the other hand, anyone who was mentally ill, a 'lunatic', was to have his land restored to him by the Crown when he recovered.

At this time the practices of society towards people with a mental handicap varied. Some were restrained to ensure they caused no harm; some were placed in residential facilities such as workhouses, monasteries, prisons or hospitals; others roamed the streets as beggars or village idiots; while still others were bought by the rich to provide amusement. In the nineteenth century the growth of institutions provided a golden opportunity for studying possible causes of mental impairment. Several different forms of mental handicap were identified but the real causes remained obscure. The blame was often placed on the parents where combinations of such things as drunkenness, anxiety about being a good wife, attempted abortion or masturbation were believed to lead to a child's being impaired. Many of the social problems of the time were viewed as not only the cause of mental impairment but also partly as a direct result of people having such impairments. The view that working-class, poor people were more likely to produce children of low ability was based largely on inaccurate anecdotal evidence and led to a fear that future generations of British people would become less and less able.

Darwin's theory of evolution indicated how important inherited features were for the evolution and survival of the species and at the same time psychologists studying individual differences provided evidence that individuals who were considered to be talented or successful were most likely to come from successful families. The development of tests to measure intelligence produced the concept of the intelligence quotient (IQ) which was argued to be a measure of an individual's fixed potential. IQ tests were first used in France in the early twentieth century to determine which children would not be able to benefit from education, because of their low level of inherited intelligence. In Britain people with an IQ of less than 50 were labelled 'ineducable' and excluded from education. They were believed to be more appropriately catered for by medical staff

and were admitted to colonies or other institutions f
total care. This whole social move was supported by legislat..
in the 1913 Mental Deficiency Act which introduced compulsory admission to institutions for people who were labelled
'mentally defective'. Many people were committed for display-
ing socially unacceptable behaviour such as petty crime or
having an illegitimate child. These various influences led to the
eugenics movement which sponsored the belief that improvement in the race depended on reducing the number of children
born to 'intellectually inferior' parents. The lingering belief in
the animal nature of intellectually impaired people along with
the corresponding view that they were promiscuous and more
likely to have children, provided sufficient evidence to justify
segregation, isolation of the sexes and even sterilisation. This
segregation was also justified on the grounds that society was
thus protected from the socially unacceptable, criminal and
dangerous behaviour of people with a mental handicap.

Another product of the times was the classification of mentally handicapped people according to their apparent similarities with more 'primitive' ethnic groups. Langdon-Down,
medical superintendent of a large asylum in England, proposed
several ethnic categories, including Mongolian, Malay,
Ethiopian, Aztec and Negroid. He believed that children who
could be labelled in this way had inherited non-European features of those races which could be assumed to be farther back
on the evolutionary scale and were thus more 'animal-like' in
their nature. It is easy today to recognise how misguided these
ideas were, but the limited knowledge and social climate of the
time must have made them seem very plausible. It is only fair to
note that Down intended his work to show the clearly inherited
nature of mental handicap in order to help relieve parents and
others of any blame or guilt.

With the setting-up of the National Health Service in 1948
the colonies were transformed into 'mental subnormality hospitals' overnight. These became the responsibility of medical
superintendents, leading to an even stronger belief that people

with a mental handicap were sick patients in need of medical treatment, unlike other people of a similar age who needed education and social care.

The growth of these total institutions (Chapter 10), isolated from society, pervaded by an atmosphere of hopelessness and away from public scrutiny produced the conditions necessary for a gradual decline in the standards of care. Poor staffing, a continuing belief in the animal nature of people with a mental handicap and the statutory removal of people's rights led to abuse and dehumanisation within the institutions.

A NEW DIRECTION

The Royal Commission, set up in 1954 to look into the law relating to mental illness and mental deficiency, recognised that there should be a reversal of the policy which relied on institutional care towards a policy of 'community care'. Many people who were detained under the Mental Deficiency Acts of 1913 and 1927 were given the status of 'informal' admissions with the passing of the 1959 Mental Health Act, which followed from the Royal Commission. But this still did not enable many people to leave the hospitals as there was a continuing lack of money and staff to achieve such a transition. Many of the hospitals relied on their more able residents to clean wards, run the kitchens and laundry, labour on the hospital farm and care for less able residents. All of this without appropriate pay (see Chapter 12).

Inevitably, the knowledge of the terrible conditions within mental subnormality hospitals caused a scandal when it was eventually exposed by the press in the late 1960s. The revelations led to a number of enquiries and the government of the day published its policy document 'Better Services for the Mentally Handicapped' in 1971. This set the scene for the hospital population to be reduced dramatically within 20 years and for genuine attempts to be made to avoid segregation from the 'normal' community and services. It also recognised that many people with a mental handicap did not require regular 'medical' care, let alone hospitalisation, and it accepted that the local authority social services were more likely to deliver an appropriate service.

At around the same time the notion of 'normalisation' had started to influence the thinking of people providing services in countries such as Denmark and Sweden. It became popular to talk of mentally handicapped people being allowed to 'obtain an existence as close to the normal as possible' (Bank-Mikkelson, 1969) and that services should make available to people with a mental handicap 'patterns and conditions of everyday life which are as close as possible to the norms and patterns of the mainstream of society' (Nirje, 1970). These ideas influenced the statutes of the countries and thus had an impact on the services as actually delivered. The normalisation literature has blossomed over the last few years with Wolfensberger in the USA extending the definition to mean 'as much as possible the use of culturally valued means to enable/establish and/or maintain valued social roles for people' (Wolfensberger and Tullman, 1982).

Many of these basic principles had already started to influence planners and legislators. The 1959 Mental Health Act had encouraged the use of 'normal' services. The Education Act (1970) made the local education authorities responsible for the education of all children with a mental handicap, bringing them closer to using the services available to other children. The Jay Committee, which enquired into mental handicap nursing and care, produced a report in 1979 which had the potential to move services ahead dramatically. The Committee decided that 'to plan for the future [they] should go back to first principles and examine the needs [and rights] of mentally handicapped people'.

From this information they listed a set of fundamental principles around which they built a model of the way in which care should be delivered. They argued that people with a mental

ıcap should have access to all general facilities and services
any other member of the public, with specialist services
eing provided only where special needs were identified. All of
their recommendations stemmed from their 'belief in the pri-
macy of a "normal" lifestyle for mentally handicapped people'.
They also stressed the right of a person to be treated as an individual who should be involved in decisions that affected him/
her and who would have needs that were unique and which
changed over time. They recognised that the new pattern of services they recommended would demand a change in the views
and attitudes of professional staff, the community and society
as a whole, but they expressed confidence that 'a society which
recognises the dignity and worth of its most handicapped members is also likely to develop the most cost effective pattern of
service'. They were almost certainly correct but the report's implications were too daunting for professionals, resource holders
and politicians to contemplate and the report continues to
gather dust.

In a modern society there are many factors which determine
how people with a mental handicap are understood and treated.
Many of the historical issues already portrayed continue to
thread their way through the beliefs held by the general population, while the physical buildings, the people still incarcera-
ted in them and even some of the caring practices remain as
legacies from other eras. To break out of this trap it will be
necessary to bring about changes in the way people with a
mental handicap are valued by society, in legislation and the
political stance of all parties which form successive governments as well as in the way people with a handicap view themselves. The theme which runs through the more advanced
modern thinking on services for people with a mental handicap
places the individual at the centre and insists that services
should be designed to meet the individual's real needs, without
imposing isolation or segregation from the natural community.
The community, and the society of which it is a part, must help
each individual achieve a valued social role and must also there-

fore be helped positively to revalue people with a mental handicap. Only then will such people move towards genuine integration into small communities and into the life of those communities.

There are many social barriers which can prevent an individual from achieving a normal social role involving participation in the regular cultural, economic and political activities of society (Brechin et al, 1981). Many people, including the person with the handicap, hold prejudiced beliefs about mental handicap. There is a confusion between mental handicap and mental illness, with a tendency to attribute, incorrectly, a wide variety of socially unacceptable behaviour to people labelled as mentally handicapped. Personal experience can do a great deal to change these views, but even people with considerable experience and knowledge still baulk at having a person with a mental handicap as their next-door neighbour because of their own prejudices. Education and exposure to the concept of mental handicap which is based on accurate information and facts will be needed on a grand scale if prejudices are to be reduced or removed.

People in society develop a range of behaviours which actively discriminate against individuals with a mental handicap. As already noted, if the basic philosophy of a society is based on the survival of the fittest then the 'survivors' will automatically treat the less able in ways which discriminate against them. Legislation can lead to discrimination in the form of exclusion from those things most of us consider normal, such as education, employment, marriage or ownership of property.

Many features of the physical environment in a locality, in offices or factories may be designed for the average, non-handicapped person and will thus ensure, at the very least, a passive discrimination. Social barriers can be set up simply because society and its systems are standardised for use by this 'average' person for the sake of efficiency and simplicity. Finally, many people discriminate by avoiding people with a mental handicap, by treating them with false friendship or by open rejection. Much of this discriminatory behaviour develops over long periods of time and may occur without any real awareness. Strategies to help remove such deep-seated discrimination are likely to require strong inducements from society and to demand active, positive discrimination towards people with a mental handicap.

Democracy in Britain implies that elected individuals are given the responsibility for deciding which needs are most important and how those needs should be met. For minorities, such as people with a mental handicap, particularly where their voice is neither strong nor easily heard or listened to, there is a natural social barrier which will make integration more difficult. Even where services are good their availability may be restricted by limited quantity or poor accessibility. People with a mental handicap must have a voice which can genuinely influence the society on which they depend and into which they should be integrated. This will require more involvement at all levels by such individuals or by true advocates on their behalf.

REFERENCES

Bank-Mikkelson, N. E. (1969). A metropolitan area in Denmark: Copenhagen. In *Changing Patterns in Residential Services for the Mentally Retarded* (eds. Kugel, R. and Wolfensberger, W.). President's Committee on Mental Retardation Washington, D.C.

Brechin, A., Liddiard, P. and Surain, J. (eds.). (1981). *Handicap in a Social World*. The Open University, England.

Department of Education and Science (1970). *The Education (Handicapped Children) Act: Responsibility for the Education of Mentally Handicapped Children*, Circular 15/70. HMSO, London.

Department of Health and Social Security (1971). *Better Services for the Mentally Handicapped*, Cmnd. 4683. HMSO, London.

Nirje, B. (1970). The normalisation principle – implications and comments. *Journal of Mental Subnormality*, **16**, 62–70.

Report of the Committee of Enquiry into Mental Handicap Nursing and Care: the Jay Committee Report (1979). HMSO, London.

Wolfensberger, W. and Tullman, S. (1982). A brief outline of the principle of normalization. *Rehabilitation Psychology*, **27**, 131–45.

FURTHER READING

Ryan, J. and Thomas, F. (1980). *The Politics of Mental Handicap*. Penguin Books, Harmondsworth.
Scheerenberger, R. C. (1983). *A History of Mental Retardation*. Paul H. Brookes Publishing Co, Baltimore, USA.

Chapter 3
Families and Handicap

The recognition that one's child has an impairment is always devastating. The subsequent development of the child and of the family will depend greatly on the family's ways of responding to life's challenges, as well as on the child's ultimate disabilities.

Families are not fixed entities; the 'nuclear' family of two parents and their children is part of a wider kinship of three or four generations interrelated in tiers. Interactions and influences move upwards, downwards and sideways through the generations, across brothers and sisters, in-laws and cousins. Extended families develop and transmit attitudes towards relationships, responsibilities, power, possessions, sexuality, and life itself. Missing members of extended families, or a non-existent extended family, can be the focus of myths and fantasies of good or bad images to live up to. Families are dynamic networks in a state of continuous evolution. They are shaped by the experiences of their members and the fulfilment or failure of their expectations. Influences come from the arrival of new members by marriage and by births, and they always change the balance of relationships. New members of families may unknowingly provide a replacement for a lost member, family interrelationships may then attempt to mould into them the characteristics of the lost one. The possibly unrealistic expectations and hopes of one generation may have been 'failed' by their children and subsequently placed on the grandchildren.

Grandfather may look forward to his grandson's taking over the family business or a granddaughter to supply the attentive devotion the other women in his life did not provide. What families value and believe in are reflected in the ways families behave, especially in the ways they enact their roles with each other. What men are expected to do and to be (or not!), whether women are expected to be supportive but dependent, and how much adults are thought entitled to deal aggressively with children, are all clearly demonstrated in family life. The expected and permitted ways of expressing love, trust, anger and grief are similarly common and important attitudes expressed in the family and other settings.

Family beliefs, practices and traditions continue to change and evolve; some disappear or are modified, others are added. The surrounding cultural environment can greatly influence the younger generation, and as new communication technology rapidly introduces new knowledge, changes in beliefs and practices may instill new traditions very quickly. The availability of new knowledge can be important, for example, in diminishing old sources of guilt and reducing despair after the birth of a child with an impairment.

To parents, the significance of any expected birth will vary enormously. It may be much desired, for a variety of reasons: it may be felt as a mixed blessing; it may seem an absolute personal disaster; or simply another mouth to feed. Whatever is the parental view of the pregnancy, the baby is expected to be 'normal'. When a baby is born with an impairment, a mixture of emotional reactions results. The responses are fundamental and part of the human condition: how they are expressed and then dealt with subsequently are greatly influenced by the customs of the family and of surrounding society.

When a baby is born with a visible impairment, parents and others experience a sudden 'bereavement'. They grieve over the loss of the 'normal' baby they had expected and which is not to be. Mourning is a psychological and physical response to the loss of any major element in life. The loss can be a death or a limb or sight; a marriage, a career, or self-esteem. There are several well-recognised phases in the process of mourning before full adjustment to ordinary living occurs.

The first stage of grief is that of numbness, shock, denial of the loss: 'It is all a bad dream'. Then there is anger: 'Why us?', 'Whose fault is it?' Blame may be laid on doctors, somebody else or God. A phase of despair follows: 'We don't know what to do now; however shall we cope?'; 'Life will never be the same again' (which is true, but not necessarily hopeless). There is a restlessness, an urge to hunt for the lost person with sudden bouts of crying and anxiety, very similar to the anxiety of separation shown by small children or social animals. Knowing that this behaviour is irrational does not help adults in dealing with these impulses, and avoidance of grief can be a special problem for men in those cultures such as Britain, where for some reason they are not expected to express their grief openly. These stages of mourning are accompanied by various physical changes and symptoms. Finally, for most people there comes the gradual readjustment to the change to life. Sometimes individuals get stuck in certain phases and remain in a state of chronic anger or chronic despair and need help to grow past it. Any kind of major bereavement can profoundly shake a host of assumptions we make about our world. As a result we have to learn fresh ways of thinking, acting and coping with problems. Not every major loss is necessarily harmful; many people come through bereavements stronger and more mature than before.

All the phases of mourning occur following the birth of a baby that is 'different'. Those reactions are made still more complex by two other competing emotions which may vary in strength. One is an urge to reject or discard abnormal offspring (a practice recognised in many species and throughout human history): the opposite urge is a strong biological one to nurture and care for small helpless creatures, including babies. How parents and grandparents deal with the mixture of anger, despair, guilt, disappointment, rejection and protectiveness they experience, will depend greatly on the family's past experience and attitudes but also on the impact of the attitudes and knowledge of those around them at a time when the parents are suddenly emotionally very vulnerable. Most parents who had a child with, for example, Down's syndrome, a generation or more ago, from the very start underwent bad experiences including incorrect information, bad advice, professional rejection and neglect, public avoidance and shame. Those experiences moulded, and commonly left very underdeveloped, the lives of family members for a whole generation or more.

The realisation that a child has an impairment may not come immediately at birth, some other disabling conditions such as cerebral palsy, or severe communicaton or learning difficulties, may become apparent only following many months of uncertainty. Some children are born with no obvious impairment but acquire brain damage after birth from, for instance, meningitis or head injury.

When an impairment has been apparent soon after birth, many parents admit later to the feelings of rejection they had towards their impaired new baby. 'I wanted to put a pillow over her head and I wished I was dead myself. I don't feel like that about her now.' An impaired baby was not what parents wanted and such feelings are to be expected. It is very important that parents, professionals and others realise that such negative feelings are not only natural but also are not necessarily permanent.

The parents are faced with the conflicting emotions of protectiveness and rejection and their protectiveness is likely to be strengthened where those around them are emphasising and appreciating the ordinary normal characteristics of the new baby rather than his or her differences. It does not help new parents to have ward staff giving pitying glances, or paediatricians spontaneously suggesting fostering services. Such behaviours indicate a view that the new baby is somehow regrettable. By conveying their own attitudes of hopelessness and rejection, the staff can increase the parents' despair. The staff's perception of the situation is of course coloured by their past experiences, quite possibly dating back to the previous generation, and this highlights the enormous importance of training for staff in maternity units: training which will update their knowledge, explore their own perceptions and attitudes to disability, and help them to maintain positive support to newly affected parents. Staff, that is maternity staff, paediatricians, health visitors, and GPs, need to achieve the fine balance between a positive approach to the new baby while allowing and enabling the parents to grieve. Fathers can have a particularly harsh time. Often in the past fathers were told of the baby's condition and then given the task of informing the mother. It is still usual to leave the father to tell friends, neighbours and workmates. British men still cannot cope with expressions of grief by their own sex and the expected outlet for many men is simply to get drunk. Behind this wall of silence, however, fathers can experience terrible feelings of failed manhood, guilt and shame, leading sometimes to physical impotence.

The part grandparents play must not be underestimated. Their acceptance or otherwise of the new baby and its condition can strengthen or undermine the efforts of the parents to cope with their experiences. The refusal of a paternal grandparent, for example, to acknowledge a child with Down's syndrome as a full grandchild can create family tensions and sadness for years. The wholehearted support, both emotional and practical, from grandparents and the extended family, however, can be a mutually enriching experience. Those grandparents for whom the new child is a profound disappointment are grieving also: not only for the grandchild that never was, but perhaps about social issues important for their generation, such as respectability and shame. It may be for those reasons that any attempt to help them may be rebuffed.

Several studies made of parents' views show that most couples would have preferred to have been told together and with sensitivity, on the second day, about their baby's condition. Couples experience the shock and numbness of initial grief, feel anger and ask many 'why's?' In their state of shock the answers may be forgotten and the questions asked again, perhaps several times, during the next few weeks. The following months are likely to be profoundly lonely for the parents, launching unprepared on an uncharted sea. The friendship and support of parents who have recently navigated a similar journey successfully can be of immense comfort. (One parent organisation which offers support is indeed called 'Pilot Parents'.) During the first few days, then, it is appropriate for the counsellor (such as paediatrician or social worker) to enquire gently how all the grandparents and parents have taken the news, and would they like a chance to discuss it? The father may like to discuss how to handle any embarrassment neighbours may show, and both parents can be offered contact with other local parents in a similar situation.

The events of the child's first year are quite unpredictable. There may be enormous decisions to take soon after the birth, when the parents are perhaps least ready for the task. A child may have major disorders of the heart, spinal cord or digestive tract requiring surgery within the first days of life in order to survive. Among the factors to consider are the likelihood of the operation relieving that disorder, the risk to life from the operation and, most difficult of all: what will be the expected quality of life following a successful operation. Nobody can ever really answer this last question. Bringing up a child with a disability puts enormous emotional and practical demands on parents: unsupported families may pay a colossal price, even to the point of disintegration.

Paediatricians are regularly exposed to the pain of such families and to the problems a disabled child can face. Their advice to parents therefore stems from their extensive experience of the childhood years, but is rarely supplemented by a longer perspective of adult life, which may bring a later richness of its own. The child's innate claim to life has received greater attention and respect in recent years, and parental and paediatric wishes have occasionally been overruled by the law.

A frail baby with a tenuous hold on life, threatened by

infections, or seizures, forces those parents to experience frequently the imminent death of their infant: and although the child may outgrow these dangers, strong feelings of anxiety about his or her safety may be readily activated later in life, limiting the amount of adventure permitted.

The everyday care can be inordinately taxing. The process of feeding may be difficult and slow with a dissatisfied, constantly screaming baby: a normal sleep pattern may not emerge, so family and neighbours have disrupted nights: tempers and relationships become stretched until parents are utterly desperate. Such screaming, feeding and sleeping difficulties may be the only early suggestions that all is not well. Delay or failure in achieving the normal developmental milestones of smiling and sitting for example then add to the parents' anxiety, especially where no diagnosis has been made. To have a label for a disorder suggests that to some extent the condition is recognisable, the future is somewhat definable, and even if this future seems gloomy that is preferable to a totally uncharted future for some parents. With a first baby the question of developmental delay may first occur to the grandparents, who have to decide what to do about their anxieties.

The parents can therefore experience a terrible sense of failure over the needs of their baby for food and comfort, which adds to the despair of their grief. The practical help of health visitors, speech therapists and other professionals will not only overcome difficulties, but build the parents' confidence in their capacity to cope, and so ensure that despair does not become clinical depression. Before the feeding skills of speech therapists were available, parents were often compelled in desperation to seek institutional admission of their child. In other families, perhaps the uncertainty of the outcome, a lack of confidence in the paediatrician's interest, or maybe the 'hunting' of the mourned baby, led to parents' trying a world-wide variety of practitioners and 'specialists'. Usually the outcome was disappointing and worsened when the local specialist felt affronted and closed his door to the returning parents. The range and quality of early interventions available now is very different, and indeed care must be taken not to deluge families with specialists and therapeutic programmes. It is essential to recognise, however, that the parents of the *adults* now receiving services, often underwent dreadful early experiences: practical, emotional, social and professional. It is not surprising if some parents in that older age-group have a jaundiced view of society, and its agents' plans for their sons and daughters.

The routes into the educational system have increased in variety and are much less rigid. The failure of a child to achieve mainstream schooling can be another reactivation of sadness and sense of social rejection.

The 'assessment' of slow-learning and disabled children focused, until recently, on their deficiencies, a depressing and unhelpful process for parents, but with the effect on some families of making them ferocious fighters in response to professional defeatism. Again, the ways in which parents respond to the situation may reflect family traditions and attitudes to life and 'authority'.

Any family network may contain personality and relationship difficulties with tensions and friction: the practical and emotional demands added by a child's disabilities will have further impact on them. Marriages may reluctantly remain together, or be finally destroyed, around the child's needs. Often parents will evolve mutually supportive roles with great cheerfulness. The exact role of the child's problems in a distraught family needs to be identified, as old hurts, angers and disappointments may be reawakened (from the past), rather than freshly created, by the current problems. The aim of counselling for such a family is to identify ways in which a sense of success and improved perceptions of one another can be achieved. This sort of intervention can be helpful at any stage of the family's evolution, but the earlier a family acquires understanding of itself, the earlier it may resolve some difficulties.

The middle school years may be relatively quiet, between

two phases of uncertainty. Since 1971 *all* children have been entitled to education, and schools are firmly identified by families as their major source of support. Any brothers and sisters will be growing up, too, contributing to, and affected by, the life of the disabled child.

Brothers and sisters are almost inevitably required to be tolerant, to keep quiet, let mother devote much time to feeding, or reluctantly share toys to keep the peace. Games and toys may be spoilt, or homework interrupted. Children can still experience deeply hurtful teasing at school about their sibling's condition. The problems may become worse in adolescence when the behaviour of the disabled child in the home may intrude on the social life of a teenage brother or sister. The parents provide an important model here: their practical approach, or their embarrassment, sets the scene for teenage friends' responses. Before community forms of shared care existed, and institutional life was the only alternative to the family home, many parents had such a horror that their son or daughter may be 'put away' that they secured promises from their other children early in life that they would always provide a home. Those brothers and sisters unable later to keep the childhood promise have carried a sense of guilt subsequently.

Brothers and sisters, or other family members, may need counselling about the likelihood that their own children may have an impairment and this help is usually available through paediatricians and genetic clinics.

Despite tremendous practical improvements in services to school-age children and their families, there remains a serious area of neglect. Parents are still left without expectations of a truly adult role for their growing children. The assumptions remain that the future will consist of the parental home, and the Adult Training Centre (ATC) apparently designed for 'asexual and incomplete' people. Both services and society must ensure that the parents' perceptions of their child's future can be realistically improved.

With the adolescence of normal children, parents recognise

that their separation is not far away, emotional bonds are changing, their new sexuality offers hazards; the parents' own youth
is finally passed and an uncertain new phase of life lies ahead.
The significance of these developments depends on the family
and personal attitudes. When a child has a major disability,
though, adolescence raises some of those issues, but also a
rekindling of the grief about what will not be, and renewed
anxieties about the future, especially after the parents' death.

Many practical problems arise with adolescence. The
increase in body size can make physical care a heavier task.
Menstrual hygiene may be a major and regular problem. Adolescents stay up at night longer and leave parents less time to
themselves: they need escorts and transport to go anywhere.
Brothers and sisters enlarge their social world and start to leave
home, so the disabled youngster is lonely. Normal adolescents
can physically separate from their parents' presence, the disabled one cannot, and their resentment is commonly directed at
the mother in various ways.

Sexual maturity involves many issues. Parents are generally
poor at sharing sexual knowledge with normal children who
largely acquire it elsewhere. The child with severe handicaps
cannot have access to those sources, and their untutored sexual
conduct may be embarrassing and unacceptable. Parents may
worry about daughters' being exploited, but forget a son can
acquire an unsavoury reputation from his untutored innocent
explorations. The idea of sexual intimacy in the lives of people
with severe disabilities still activates deep prejudices and beliefs
about sex and sin and pleasure and power. It is often too
disturbing a subject in some families, who then deny its existence.

Most young adults have remained with their parents,
although the combination of problems around that period still
makes the early 20s the peak age for admission to residential
care. The new generation of parents has experienced support in
childhood and is rightly demanding its continuity, including
day services for all.

The more recent generation of parents who have experienced support for their children, are demanding a continuation, including local respite care and day services, for all adults. Those parents, however, are already middle aged and are still shaping their lives around ATC bus schedules and the daily needs of their sons and daughters. Older parents have had their whole lives moulded as trios, with one or other parent fully occupied in the care of the son or daughter. That, and supporting their local mental handicap society, has consumed all their energy. Eventually an elderly widowed mother may be increasingly reliant on that son or daughter to support her at home.

For many families their problems were so complex that admission of their child to hospital was the only solution. Their desperation was compounded by their sense of failure and the sadness of separation – often over great distances. They were often labelled as 'rejecting', or 'over-protective' (whatever they did) and their relationships with parents who did not have to use the hospitals has been uncomfortable. Nevertheless, those parents were grateful, and the placement was seen as a final, if not perfect, 'answer'. However, the increasing recognition that people with the severest of disabilities still grow and develop (given the right supports) now challenges that assumption, and reminds us all that living itself is an ever-changing state. But for some parents who years ago with great pain had to negotiate the 'solution' for their children, the prospect now of their grown sons' and daughters' starting on new life experiences presents an emotional and philosophical upheaval which is quite unbearable. Pressure comes from those parents to maintain the institutions.

Reference was made earlier to the variations in family styles of viewing and coping with major life events. Despite the enormous obstacles which face families with a very disabled member, most do more than survive; they develop a lifestyle, have fun, and are proud of the achievements and pleasures of their sons and daughters. There is an old folk test of attitudes to life: in viewing a pint of milk in a quart jug, is the jug perceived as half *empty* or as half *full*? Where the awareness of imperfection dominates, life becomes bleak; but the capacity to perceive any life as an adventure, releases creativity. The meaning of imperfection and pain is a question pondered by many, and a religious answer is found by some. There is a need for research of the *positive* experiences families have known from disability. The caring professions are exposed predominantly to the *sorrows* of the human condition, and find insufficient time to share the gentle joys of life and learn from those they serve.

FURTHER READING

Gallagher, J. J. and Vietze, P. M. (eds.) (1986). *Families of Handicapped Persons: Research. Programs and Policy Issues*. Paul H. Brooks Publishing Co, Baltimore, USA.

Hannam, C. (1980). *Parents and Mentally Handicapped Children*. Penguin Books, Harmondsworth.

MacKeith, R. (1973). The feelings and behaviour of parents of handicapped children. *Developmental Medicine and Child Neurology*. **15**, 24–7.

Chapter 4
Assessment

The words 'assessment', 'test' and 'examination' all seem to carry similar meanings. For most people they conjure up memories which include uncertainty, anxiety or even fear: they have often been associated with the notion that one is being checked out to see if one is good enough at something or whether there is some defect in some particular personal attribute. Assessment regularly seems to carry with it a comparison of one's own results with the results obtained by other people which may lead in turn to the individual's feeling less than perfect or, worse still, not even average. There are many specific assessments which can be used, but it is not the intention of this chapter to look at these in detail. It is most important, before considering any specific assessment, to have a broad understanding of the process and to set up a system within which assessment can take place. To try to see what assessment is actually about it may be helpful to consider some of the factors which underlie its use.

In proposing a mechanism for assessment, it is important to recognise that human beings are incredibly complex. The truth is that we understand less about human beings than we understand about most other subjects. The process of assessment should be used to help us. In our everyday lives we use assessment regularly, sometimes to attempt to estimate the worth or value of something, sometimes to try to estimate how likely it is that a particular thing will happen. We use it to form general impressions about people or perhaps to make judgements about them. When we meet someone for the first time we assess them, and often make important decisions based upon our first impressions. As human beings have gradually developed and have attempted to improve the world, a whole new science of assessment has been developed. People like psychologists and sociologists spend considerable time in producing better ways to obtain more precise information about people and what they do. The process of assessment has become more complicated and technical and when someone we know is assessed, perhaps by a particular professional or worse still by a team of people, it seems almost impossible to know what is being done or what the results mean.

In attempting to understand assessments there are four simple processes that most people go through which are worth remembering: description, prediction, explanation and control.

1. DESCRIPTION

First, from a very early age we learn to describe the world that is around us and within us. We are taught ways of telling others and ourselves what we see, hear and feel. For the most part society agrees specific labels for the various pieces of information that reach us through our senses and we then use those labels to communicate with each other. This process of description is often the first stage in any assessment.

2. PREDICTION

Second, people attempt to discover ways of making the world as predictable as possible. Many things are so predictable that one comes to rely on them and to put a great deal of faith and trust in them. This applies not only to things but also to people. It is possible to become so used to something or someone being predictable that even a small change in it can upset a routine and even put lives at risk. The second phase of assessment involves using this idea of predictability to make judgements, based upon any information we can gather, about what the future is likely to hold for an individual. Many of the assessments which have become accepted are designed to help predict how an individual will progress, say in school or in a job.

3. EXPLANATION

Third, people try to understand their world by finding explanations for what has happened. Human beings like to have reasons why things have happened. There are dozens of explanations for people's behaviour in our everyday language. One may agree that 'he raided the fridge because he was hungry' or one may accept that 'she was upset with her boyfriend because she was jealous'. One may explain that 'he failed his exams because he was lazy'. Where possible, attempts are made to ensure that the explanations stay within the limits of what is known and understood about the world. But often, particularly with human behaviour, one's understanding is so poor that the explanations go beyond the facts. In the process of assessment, the search for explanations for what is observed goes on. As people become better at providing explanations it is often possible to prevent the development of such problems in the future.

4. CONTROL

The fourth important element in the process of assessment is that of control. As people get better at *describing, predicting* and *explaining* what they experience so they improve in their efforts to control things and the world becomes safer or more comfortable for them. From the moment of birth, and maybe before, the behaviour and lives of individuals are controlled or determined by many things. Society relies on the fact that individuals can be controlled by the world and the people around them, so that learning can occur. Parents, teachers, governments, and so on, help people to change as they grow up. Some of that change is beneficial, some of it may cause hardship or disability. In turn, individuals control the world around them, including the other people in their lives. Much of the control people exert over each other is very subtle, as when an individual reacts to changes in someone's facial expression or in their tone of voice. This search for control is a central part of the assessment process. It is the part which leads to action, not only to improve a particular individual's life, but also to try to prevent similar problems occurring for other individuals in the future.

To summarise: in trying to understand what happens in an assessment it is useful to recognise that the assessors, who should include the individual themselves, are invariably trying to *describe* an individual and what they do so that they can *predict* and *explain* the behaviour or its absence with the hope that they can help the individual to change through some method of *control*. This implies that before any detailed assessments, such as intelligence tests, language assessments or skills inventories are carried out, it is necessary to develop a *system* within which any individual can benefit from assessment.

THE ASSESSMENT PROCESS

Keeping these four factors in mind, it should be possible to design a system within which the needs of an individual can be identified and as far as possible met. At the centre of every assessment is the individual who is to be assessed. From the outset that individual should be involved with every decision and every part of the assessment. Where individuals are unable to make their own decisions someone close to them should be able to talk and act on their behalf. The person, or his representative should first be able to choose whether he wishes to be assessed and then be able to take part in any assessment as an equal partner with others who carry out the assessment. This process is not easy and it places stresses and strains on both the individual and the assessors. This implies that the person, his representative and the professionals need to work closely together to help each other understand the purpose of assessments and what the outcome might be. Where they are asked to take part in meetings, the individual and his representative should understand who the other members of the team are, their roles and what is expected to happen at the meeting. They should be offered an opportunity to be given support by someone who already knows the 'system', and who has also had the opportunity to get to know them well. The atmosphere must be such that the individual can feel totally free to participate in what should be a decision-making process about his/her own life.

Broad-based assessment

In trying to understand someone's life with them it is essential to have an opportunity to get to know him, his background, and what his life is like today. Having someone look closely at one's life can be difficult and sometimes painful. This requires a considerable amount of tact and understanding on the part of those helping to carry out an assessment. Life is made up of many complicated areas, which include having a place to live, an education, an occupation which provides a living wage, time and opportunities for leisure, and good quality health care when it is required. It is also important to consider the individual's social and spiritual needs. Each of these areas of life is extremely complex and can include many things which most people would find difficult to share with others. A further complication is that much of the information for an assessment can only be gathered by talking with other people in the person's life. Neighbours, relatives, friends, employers, and so on, may all be valuable contributors at this stage. Once again great care and sensitivity is required on the part of the assessor. At different times in a person's life particular areas will become more important. For example, if someone is about to leave full-time education, the area of occupation and regular work will take on a much greater significance. It is easy to be led into concentrating on one specific area which seems vital, with other areas being ignored. At this first stage it is worth trying to maintain a broad view in helping individuals to review their lives and to determine their main needs. This form of broad assessment should be designed to help each person consider what life is like for them today, what relationships exist for them, what happens in their life throughout the day, evening, overnight and at weekends, and finally, what opportunities and experiences they require in the main areas of their life.

Teamwork

Anyone who joins with the person at this stage of assessment, requires considerable skills in learning to relate to the person, as well as an ability to work with others. Where several people are closely involved in such an assessment it is likely that they will have to meet on at least one occasion as a team. Such a team will work best in an atmosphere of co-operation and trust. Although such a meeting may be a fairly formal occasion, all team members will find it easier to participate in the right atmosphere. Ideally, people should come to the meeting with information to share so that sensible decisions can be taken to help the individual progress. It is often the case that the more people who attend the meeting, the more difficult it is to obtain agreement on anything. The best method to achieve agreement is to accept that it requires a consensus and to work towards that.

Consensus decision-making

The idea of consensus decision-making has recently come

under critical scrutiny, particularly in terms of the management of services, but at the level of decisions made about an individual's life, where the individual has the right to be closely involved in every decision, the consensus method has clear advantages. Decisions taken through the assessment process have a direct and important impact on the quality of life and service offered to the person with a mental handicap. They can also affect the degree to which the person is able to participate as a citizen in the community in which he or she lives. In a consensus decision-making process, each member of the team, including the person with a mental handicap, has an equal opportunity to influence decisions, which must be agreed by everyone present.

Such a process requires enough time to gather and share information and for discussion of various opinions and options. Very often the information gathered can be complex and requires careful interpretations from various standpoints. Where a variety of people from different backgrounds are available, the interpretation of the information is likely to be complex but potentially more valuable. A mechanism for generating possible solutions to the identified needs and some way of determining what is an acceptable solution are required. Decisions reached at this stage by consensus are more likely to give each member a strong feeling of commitment to acting upon the decision and to achieving the desired aim. In some cases a consensus may be difficult to achieve; where this is so it is possible to agree a number of alternatives, which can be tried and evaluated.

Where team members have agreed to the use of a consensus decision-making process, and have received some training in it, it is likely that there will be very few occasions when agreement cannot be reached. However, in the event of a failure to reach agreement, some mechanism of appeal may be required. Such a mechanism should ensure that even the least powerful members of the team feel completely at liberty to challenge any decision which they feel unable to support. The appeals mechanism should be such that each team member has confidence in its operation and is prepared to agree to abide by any decision made through the appeal. In practice, some decisions about any individual's life are likely to be complex and will necessarily involve informed guesses and value judgements. There is no easy way through this and the consensus decision-making process offers a mechanism which should permit high quality decisions which are not seen to be irrevocable.

Although people may have views on what the outcome should be before they go to the meeting, it is important to remain flexible. Where various opinions and options are proposed there must be time for proper discussion of these. It is not always the most obvious option which is necessarily the best. The team will need to select what they feel is the best solution and to consider what alternatives might be available in the event of that solution's failing. Ideally the outcome of the meeting should be recorded so that as each area of a person's life is addressed, the decisions taken about what opportunities and experiences are needed in that area are noted.

Choosing priorities

Although a number of areas may be identified which require some action, not all of these goals are likely to be achievable at once. It is important to help the individual to choose which area, or areas, should be the first priorities. Judging which is the most important overall need to be met must depend heavily on the individual and his life as a whole. The most important need may be something which will only be achieved in the future. In order to meet that particular need there may be a number of shorter-term goals which have to be set. For example, if everyone agrees that the most important thing for a person is to obtain somewhere to live as independently as possible, then it would be possible to set a variety of short-term goals which would lead to that eventual aim. The person may need help to register himself on a housing list, to look into which area he would prefer to live and to begin to assess his own life in more detail, so that he is gradually enabled to make a move.

It is also important to ask whether it is actually feasible to meet the identified needs. An affirmative answer may depend upon the team's being creative, and finding ways to use the available resources imaginatively. On the other hand it may prove to be impossible to meet the need because of limited resources, and it is important to make this recognition and have some mechanism to inform the management and planning systems of such deficiencies.

Service deficiencies

Those who plan the service system and those who control directly the available resources need to be made aware, clearly and accurately, of any service deficiency. Any service that sets out to become capable of meeting the real needs of individuals as they are identified, must have some mechanism to monitor gaps in its ability to meet those needs. The more clearly the needs can be described the more likely it is that the service required can be accurately identified. It would be naïve to believe that the process of identifying the type of service needed will automatically enable it to be provided. If, however, a mechanism can be developed that will ensure that all the deficiencies are recorded, it should be possible for planners and those who control the resources to put priorities on developments and to make sure that they really do meet the needs of known individuals.

It is clear that service developments in the past have not been designed to meet the particular needs of individuals and invariably they have offered a compromise system into which many individuals have had to be fitted. Obviously a change towards a service system designed around each individual person will not occur overnight. It is likely that extra resources will be needed, but it is imperative that this does not prevent people aspiring towards such a system. At the centre of such a system must be a broad-based, regular, accurate, and sensitive process of assessment for each individual.

Individual plans

Even detailed and accurate assessments will be of little value unless there is also a mechanism for putting recommendations into action. The mechanism to do this needs to be relatively simple and usable even within a service which is under pressure and with limited resources. Having set priorities through the broad-based assessment process, these must be translated into statements of action. Each priority task should be specified in such a way that everyone will know who must do what to achieve that task. The person or persons who accept responsibility for any particular task must also agree a target date for completing it and be very clear what is required of them. When each priority task has an individual name and a clear action stated against it, this will form the basis of an Individual Plan. This plan must be recorded very clearly so that even people not present at the meeting are able to understand what is required and to judge whether or not it is achieved. This mechanism not only monitors the action and its achievement, but also enables any failure to be recorded and analysed. The reasons for failure can then be used either to set out further steps to try to achieve the goal or to identify the service deficiency which prevented the achievement. It is clear that further, more detailed assessments perhaps from specialist workers may be required at different stages throughout the person's life, but the broad-based assessment process with its annual review and the individual planning mechanism should identify these needs.

Important functions

There are at least two functions which must be carried out if this assessment process is to work. First, somebody must operate as a 'key worker'. Such an individual should have regular contact with the person, should be in a position to work with that person towards meeting his needs and most importantly be acceptable to him. In principle the key worker could be any person closely involved in the individual's life. The role would be to support the person with a mental handicap at assessment meetings, to help those meetings develop an appropriate description of the individual's needs and plan of action, and to take an active part in the implementation of that plan. Where possible, they should become a stable part of the person's life so that close relationships, so necessary in all our lives, are not disturbed. It is obvious that the key worker may need to change, but this should only occur where the individual receiving the service requests such a change, where the key worker leaves the area and is no longer available, or where the service being offered changes such that there is a more logical person available to carry out the key worker role. Determining who the key worker is going to be is not a decision about professional boundaries or formal status within the system, but must be based upon the identified needs of the individual and, where possible, upon his choice.

The second function that can be clearly identified is that of a 'co-ordinator'. When any mechanism is set up to help a person identify his needs and to have them met it is clear that this will range across a various and changing set of services. In the early years of an individual's life, the *health services* may be the main provider. As he grows up *education* will play a more central role and later on services providing *residential, social* and *occupational* support may become more prominent. In order to ensure close liaison and co-ordination between such services, it is vital to have one individual operate in a co-ordinating role. There is clearly no one professional group or organisation currently set up to carry out this role. Many people at present act as co-ordinators; calling meetings, chairing those meetings and ensuring that decisions are taken and recorded. The important thing is to ensure that the function of co-ordinator is recognised and that somebody is nominated to carry it out. Most teams eventually nominate somebody for the role, but this does not ensure that the person has the necessary skills to carry it out. The co-ordinator must be able to act as a facilitator within the team and to have the skills to resolve conflicts as they arise. Such conflicts can be a positive part of team decision-making and can lead to genuine consensus with a true commitment from all team members.

SUMMARY

There are many different reasons for carrying out assessments with an individual. Assessment is often used to describe an individual and what he can do, or it may be necessary to compare one person with others in order to see what special problems he may be having. As people grow up and their lives change, assessment can often help identify their real needs and which of these are most important. From these needs it may be possible to assess what is required to meet them. For example, where it is possible to identify some service that might help the individual overcome a particular problem then that service can be made available. Where there is no such service available this deficiency can be identified and the information used by planners to help determine what services are needed for the future. Broad-based assessments can be used to inform other professions who may then carry out specialised, more detailed assessments. Still further assessments may take place to help measure the individual's progress.

At each stage assessment must be linked to some form of action. Gathering information is only useful if it leads to sensible decisions and positive change. This chapter has emphasised the necessity for a co-ordinated system within which the process of assessment can take place and has offered an outline of such a process.

FURTHER READING

Hersen, M., Kazdin, A. E. and Bellack, A. S. (eds.). (1983). *The Clinical Psychology Handbook*. Pergamon Press Inc, New York.

Matson, J. L. and Mulick, J. A. (eds.). (1983). *Handbook of Mental Retardation*. Pergamon Press Inc, New York.

Chapter 5
The Role of the Physiotherapist, Occupational Therapist and Speech Therapist

by S. R. Bell MCSP, H. Berry LCST and
S. Hubbard DipCOT

The assessment process attempts to identify the individual needs of the client in all areas of his/her life, which may involve the intervention of professionals from various disciplines. Therapists should be seen as integral members of the multidisciplinary team, seeking to meet those needs and helping to provide an overall holistic approach to the person.

Each of the therapy professions offers particular skills and expertise which complement each other, yet they do have areas of overlap. In this chapter an attempt is made to explain the common aim while acknowledging differences and similarities.

PHYSIOTHERAPY

Physiotherapists who deal with people who have a mental handicap will work with clients who have both physical and non-physical needs. As members of a multidisciplinary team, physiotherapists are involved in the identification of these needs using specialist assessments which examine physical

57

problems and they participate in the broader, general assessment which looks at the whole client, his lifestyle, and future needs.

Some of the goals which are identified in the individual plan will be the responsibility of the physiotherapist to fulfill. This may mean using techniques such as passive movements, hydrotherapy and positioning, or using the developing newer methods, such as rebound/trampolining therapy and vibration therapy.

Physiotherapists will also be involved with clients who have little or no obvious physical problems. A major area of involvement will be in development of leisure and recreation. The institutional life of a long-stay hospital may limit a client's capacity to make choices. Physiotherapists can use their skills to enable clients to sample a wide range of physical activities and movement and thereby help establish a true basis for choice. In so doing, they help the client develop positive self-image, an awareness of bodily health, and a general feeling of well-being in meeting new and exciting challenges through participation. The physiotherapist's knowledge and understanding of kinesiology and recreational therapy has an important role to play in developing the potential of a person with a mental handicap in this area.

The physiotherapist, as a team member, must also identify the level of support needed from this service to meet the agreed goals. This involves deciding upon a long-term, short-term, or advisory commitment to the client. However, much work of an advisory nature is also undertaken with the client's carers. This involves numerous areas, from teaching lifting and handling skills to developing muscle-strength building programmes. At this level, a knowledge of seating, particularly in wheelchairs, is important as many clients will have physical problems affecting their posture and balance. Advice to carers on appropriate seating ensures not only the client's comfort, but helps prevent a physical problem from deteriorating. In the same way, the physiotherapist will need to advise on footwear and walking aids.

The specialist physiotherapist in mental handicap may not

always be the appropriate person to achieve the set goal. If the client has an acute condition outside the mental handicap, such as a sports injury, then he/she should receive treatment from a physiotherapist with that expertise. This may involve attendance at an outpatient department or a visit from the generic community physiotherapist.

It is important to have a physiotherapy service flexible enough to be client-centred rather than service-centred. Physiotherapists will, therefore, be involved in all locations where clients live and work, including Adult Training Centres (ATCs), hostels and the client's own home. This may also mean not working a rigid nine-to-five routine but implementing a flexi-time system.

The physiotherapist, above all, should be working as a member of a multidisciplinary team, striving with colleagues of other disciplines to meet the identified needs of clients, by using his own particular skills and expertise.

OCCUPATIONAL THERAPY

Occupational therapy is the treatment of physical and psychiatric conditions through specific activities, helping people reach their maximum level of function and independence in all aspects of daily life. The approach is 'holistic' and aims to habilitate wherever possible and assist in adjustment where conditions are deteriorating, while at all times considering the quality of life.

Occupational therapists work closely with all other health and social service professions – there will be many skills in common – but there are specific skills which an occupational therapist can bring to the team.

The key to the development of a therapeutic programme is accurate assessment and definition of individual objectives. The occupational therapist will specifically cover all the aspects of daily living – including self-care, domestic, employment and social skills – which make up the ability of an individual to meet the demands of integrated living; in addition, an assessment of the personal ability to communicate effectively, to make appropriate use of leisure time, to manage money, to use community resources and to modify behaviour according to circumstances, must all be established if a picture of the individual is to be created and an understanding reached of the particular needs.

Having defined needs and abilities, the occupational therapist will with her colleagues develop programmes designed to maximise ability and minimise *dis*-ability.

The four prime areas (domestic, social, work and leisure skills) encompass communication and education processes. The skills needed to achieve competence in these areas are sensori-motor, cognitive, intrapersonal and interpersonal. Occupational therapy techniques are designed to promote the development and maintenance of these skills. Skills already acquired need only be re-learned if they are maladaptive, but those not already learned to the necessary level of competence for functional performance will require to be taught. Skills will fade if not used, so only those skills are taught which the individual needs to achieve functional independence or adjustment within his environment. All of this goes a long way towards developing self-esteem and self-awareness, as well as improving self-expression and interest.

Occupational therapy departments are generally staffed with a mixture of people from differing backgrounds, some of whom will be occupational therapists, all bringing their own specific skills. Some of the departments' work will be with individuals on a one-to-one basis, other activities will take place as part of a group. Activities such as social skills, literacy and numeracy skills, communication skills, etc., can all be undertaken in a group whose membership is at broadly similar levels of development and who develop a group identity in an atmosphere of mutual respect. Activities such as music, pottery and woodwork can provide an excellent medium in which to develop teamwork, skills, communication and group tolerance.

With any multidisciplinary work, co-ordination of effort and uniformity of approach are essential elements and should involve all those caring for the individual, for habilitation should be a 24-hour concept if it is to have the greatest effect.

SPEECH THERAPY

Over recent years the emphasis in work on communication, particularly with people with a mental handicap, has been in providing a functional communication system which allows the individual to interact effectively in a variety of settings. The speech therapist should be involved in looking at the client's present communicative status and the effects of his communication on his environment.

The aim of therapy must always be to provide adequate skills for interaction, even at a very basic level, and to allow the individual as much influence over his own life as possible. It is now considered that the starting point for language development is a need to communicate and that language is acquired in order to express the individual's own intentions and meanings for example, to effect actions, ask for something, protest, attract attention (Bates, 1976; Bruner, 1975). Within many institutional settings, there often appears little reason to communicate and the first step may be to heighten the awareness of carers to their own role in developing language skills. Speech therapists have a role in explaining the nature of two-way communication involving a speaker and a listener and in demonstrating how language used to the client should be effective, delivered at the right level and in the right medium, e.g. signing.

Formal and informal assessment is designed to give an overall picture of the client's communicative skills – level of comprehension, both in structured situations and with contextual cues; structure and functional use of expressive language and the articulation of speech itself. Other abilities will also be noted, such as eye contact, attention, imitation, and information gained through observation of the client's communication in his 'normal' environment and discussion with care staff, relatives and instructors. It is important to ensure that feeding problems are thoroughly assessed, and further investigation of other specific problems may be necessary – hearing, dental, voice.

Having assessed current skills and agreed aims related to the individual's needs, 'therapy' can be offered in a number of ways. There is certainly a place for structured teaching of language at all levels – from response to sound to conversational skills. These skills must then be generalised across a variety of situations and should not be seen as isolated activities. For example, the Makaton sign 'drink' can be taught along behavioural lines using immediate rewards; it must then be extended to enable the client to ask for a drink at tea-time. This generalisation, as with other abilities, is probably the hardest step, but awareness by others of the need to reinforce new skills is a major factor.

For many clients, indirect therapy is a better alternative whereby carers are involved in following through programmes on a daily basis in situations in which communication readily occurs: the home and workplace. Here, training plays an important part, and the therapist should be able to link language work into other activities. Guidelines which can be clearly understood are essential.

The use of aids for communication is an expanding area, whether it is signing (Makaton) which is being considered or a symbol-based system (Rebuss, Bliss, traditional orthography), linked to a computer or electronic aid. Close co-operation with other departments will be required to ensure all physical aspects of an alternative communication system are appropriate, and both the client and carers will need specific instruction in the effective use of any aid.

A client's ability to communicate, thereby making choices to influence his environment, is a bonus to any community-living programme. While the speech therapist provides the specialised knowledge, it is only effective if taken up by all those working with the client.

In order to offer a meaningful service to people with mental handicap, therapists must, with their medical and nursing colleagues, adopt a 'holistic' approach which offers more realistic opportunities for skills' training and life-skills' experience. No service should ignore the valuable contribution made by the statutory services, the voluntary sector, family and friends.

Therapists must not remain professionally segregated while arguing the merits of an integrated service for its users; and they must encourage all colleagues to adopt a similar approach.

REFERENCES

Bates, E. (1976). *Language and Context*. Academic Press, New York.
Bruner, J. S. (1975). Ontogenesis of speech acts. *Journal of Child Language*, 2, 1–19.

FURTHER READING

Capie, A. C. M., Taylor, P. D. and Perkins, E. A. (1980). *Teaching Basic Behavioural Principles: A Manual for Course Tutors using 'Helping the Retarded'*. British Institute of Mental Handicap, Kidderminster, England.
Clarke, D. (1982). *Mentally Handicapped People – Living and Learning*. Baillière Tindall, London.
Hallas, C. H., Fraser, W. I. and Macgillvray, R. C. (1982). *The Care and Training of the Mentally Handicapped*. Wright PSG, Bristol.
Jeffree, D.M. and McConkey, R. (1976). *Let Me Speak*. Souvenir Press, London.
Perkins, E. A., Taylor, P. D. and Capie, A. C. M. (1980). *Helping the Retarded – A Systematic Behavioural Approach*. British Institute of Mental Handicap. Kidderminster, England.
Reed, K. and Sanderson, S. (1983). *Concepts of Occupational Therapy*. Williams and Wilkins, Baltimore USA.

Warren, B. (1981). *Drama Games for Mentally Handicapped.* MENCAP, London.

Westmacott, E. V. S. and Cameron, R. J. (1981). *Behaviour Can Change.* Macmillan Educational, London.

SPECIFIC INTEREST GROUPS

The Association of Chartered Physiotherapists in Mental Handicap
Contact: Mr S. R. Bell MCSP, 23 Treswell Crescent, Hillsborough, Sheffield S6 2LE

Occupational Therapists Special Interest Group
Contact: Miss M. Bosworth DipCOT, Royal Earlswood Hospital, Redhill, Surrey RH1 6JL

Speech Therapists Special Interest Group
Contact: Mrs L Tierney LCST, Chief Speech Therapist, Highbury Hospital, Bulwell, Nottingham NG6 9DR

Chapter 6
Education

From an early age education services play a crucial role in most people's lives. The nursery class or infant school may be the first experience of extended separation from mother and home. From that point on much of each child's future, including skills, knowledge, interests and even accent, is determined by teachers and other children. For some their educational experience will revolve around special education.

One interpretation of the development of special education derives from the historical perspective of developments in society as a whole. As society became increasingly industrialised so the requirement for a productive workforce grew. It was important for this workforce to conform with certain basic standards and the normal educational system evolved to ensure that there was a consistent supply of obedient workers who could undertake the range of tasks required to guarantee production. Individuals who could not, or would not, conform to the demands of the classroom threatened not only their own future in society but also the future of their classmates who were held back by their presence. Several groups of children emerged as problems for schools and this included children with a mental handicap. In the 1880s there was a growth of special provisions for children with various types of handicap. By the 1890s local education authorities were allowed to create special schools or classes for children who were incapable of benefiting from teaching in ordinary schools because of their 'mental defect'.

Government grants were available for such special education. The Mental Deficiency Acts of 1913 and 1914 made it a duty for local education authorities to determine the mental ability of all school-age children and to provide appropriate special education for those selected as 'defective' but 'educable'.

In the nineteenth century the medical profession was struggling to gain professional status and in that struggle 'as part of the bargain' medical staff acquired the oversight of the education of people labelled 'mentally defective'. This domination by medical staff continued through the development of the large asylums, where until the 1970s there were medical superintendents in control, and even now medical officers play a key role in the 'ascertainment' of children for special education.

The development of tests of intelligence around this time enabled each individual to be assigned an intelligence quotient (IQ) as a description of his or her potential and to be compared and contrasted with everyone else. There were many arguments about the nature of intelligence. One strongly held view (Burt, 1917) was that a child's general intelligence quotient remained constant, having been determined innately, which made it possible to predict an individual's ultimate intellectual capacity. He believed that separate special schools could provide the special curriculum and conditions that were required for less able children to be educated for a useful role in life.

This use of psychological tests to determine whether or not an individual would benefit from normal education brought the psychology profession gradually into prominence. Educational psychologists are now established as a crucial part of the process by which children move from normal to special education. A referral for assessment is usually made by the head teacher who has established, using the views of her staff and her own experienced judgement, that the individual is failing to attain expected standards or that he or she is disruptive. The educational psychologist is most likely to work within a scientific framework using standardised tests to determine an individual's current ability and specific areas of deficit or problems.

It can be argued that the development of the special education system is the 'result of decisions on the part of individuals or groups with power, who control resources which they can give or withhold' (Tomlinson, 1982). These individuals or groups usually represent political or professional interests or they may be motivated by social or economic pressures.

The Warnock Committee set up to look at 'Special Educational Needs' in Britain (Warnock, 1978) assumed that about 1 in 6 children at any time, and 1 in 5 children at some time during their schooling, would need special education of some kind. This assumption was based on evidence from social surveys in different parts of the country. However the history of this society's evolving views on mental handicap (Chapter 2) shows that at different times the definitions of mental handicap and special needs and the ways they have been interpreted have changed. Surveys undertaken in the twentieth century in Britain appear to have demonstrated an increasing number of people with a handicap, both physical and mental. It is clear that such surveys are largely dependent upon the currently accepted social norms of behaviour and the derived categories and definitions which are then used to allocate individuals to groups requiring special treatment and education. The figures resulting from these surveys can be used as powerful evidence by professional or political groups to argue for increased or different resources. Thus great care is needed in interpreting survey results.

It is probably fair to assume that over time there are changes which lead to the re-assessment of the role of an educational system in society. The Council of Europe, with 21 member states including the United Kingdom, was set up in 1949 to look at a wide range of matters such as human rights, legal co-operation, the protection of natural resources, education and culture. In a project entitled 'Preparation for Life', the Council set out to identify how young people could be helped by education 'to take a full and responsible part in their social and working lives and equip them with skills and knowledge necessary to improve their changing situations' (Stobart, 1984). They concluded that all young people should be given the opportunity to acquire attitudes, knowledge and skills in four key areas.

First they should be prepared for personal life by learning to understand and respect other people, show initiative in changing situations, be able to resolve conflict in both family and community relations and deal with media information in a discriminating way. Second they should be prepared for life in a democratic society. They should understand human rights and the responsibilities of citizenship and work with others for peace. Third they should be prepared for cultural life by introduction to a range of spiritual, scientific, historical and cultural experiences. Finally they should be prepared for the world of work. The project recommended that all young people should be offered a job, further education or training as a right when compulsory schooling was complete. These conclusions were based upon the recognition that there were many challenges to which schools and young people had to respond, including high unemployment, rapidly emerging technologies, changes in family life, the impact of the media, the growth of multicultural societies and frightening challenges to democratic life.

The report argued that this preparation for adult life could be best achieved through practical experience of the values and skills outlined. Clearly such experience could not be gained purely through classroom teaching and young people needed regular contacts with the local community, work settings and social and cultural activities.

INTEGRATION

There appear to be many arguments which can be advanced for maintaining special schools. Grouping individuals with a handicap under one roof for their education means that any modifications to the building will benefit several children. The teachers working together on the same site can support each other and share their expertise. Special transport can be used to maximum effect and specialist professional staff can spend more time with the pupils and teachers instead of travelling between several schools. It is possible to bring together in one building all the special services required to meet the needs of the pupils. Few, if any, of these arguments can be traced back as an attempt to meet the genuine needs of the individual child, but, following from the above outline of the conclusions reached by the Council of Europe, it seems clear that there are several advantages or benefits to be gained from the integration of all pupils into the regular educational system. It is much easier to learn to understand and respect people with disabilities if there are regular opportunities for contact and social interaction.

People become familiar with each other and this can reduce or prevent the development of the fears that can exist about disabilities. The learning through modelling which occurs naturally between children as peers is also likely to benefit. Where children with special needs are grouped and segregated the range of behaviours available to them as models is likely to be restricted and to include a higher proportion of age-inappropriate behaviours. Individuals with a mental handicap are much more likely to be prepared for the world of work and for an ordinary cultural life in integrated settings which include the full range of age-appropriate cultural experiences.

Whereas in the past the pressures were for the segregation of problem individuals the trend more recently has been to advocate the integration of all children in a single educational system. There is now a growing understanding that there is a difference between *doing away with segregation* and *obtaining integration* (Donder and York, 1984; Education Act, 1981). Segregation can be removed simply by placing pupils in ordinary schools with peers of their own age covering the complete ability range. Children with a mental handicap may still be taught for much of the time in separate classrooms but they are not physically segregated from their non-handicapped peers. Such de-segregation does not, however, guarantee that integration will occur. Integration depends on regular, positive social interactions between all the children who are age peers. Much of the impetus for such integration is likely to have to come from the staff who work regularly with the handicapped children. The way these staff interact with the remainder of the school, encourage their students to interact, and provide a role model of how people with a mental handicap should be treated with respect and value, are all key factors in determining whether integration will be successful.

Biklen (1985) has offered a number of principles designed to ensure effective mainstreaming for all children regardless of their disabilities. First, he argued that integration must not be seen as an experiment which has to be evaluated and shown to be effective before society becomes committed to it. There must be a commitment to equality throughout society, including schools, industry, the high street and places of leisure. Such a commitment is necessary if equality is to be achieved in everyday life. As a basic value in our society equality may sometimes compete with other values but this should not lead to the total abandonment of any of these values. The decisions we take often require us to balance the various values to achieve the best outcome. Obviously such outcomes can be measured by science and this may point to ways of doing things even better. Science is unlikely, however, to tell us whether integration is right or wrong. Integration must be seen as something which is normal and must be 'institutionally guaranteed' through the stated educational policies and the planning processes which help put policy into practice.

Second, people with a mental handicap should be able to break free from their association with images that connote pity, compassion and charity. The images that go with a genuinely valued role in society involve 'activism, rights and equity'. Very often the biggest problem faced by people is not the actual disabilities but the 'stereotyping prejudice and discrimination' they suffer because of their disabilities. The process of recognising people with a mental handicap as competent individuals with equal rights and value is at the heart of the concept of 'normalization' (Wolfensberger, 1980). Biklen argues that within the world of education this means treating people with a mental handicap 'as normally as possible' by using teaching methods that are as typical as possible. Building on this view he states his third principle that 'normalization must become part of everyday life'. Society must come to offer wide support for the concept if the work done by schools is to have a real impact. People must learn to judge how they treat others by comparing it with how they would like to be treated. This is obviously difficult in a world in which many individuals feel they are themselves badly treated. When the majority of people stop discriminating against individuals with disabilities then the need to use words such as 'integration' and 'normalization' will cease.

The curricula used in special schools have undergone considerable revision since the time when the sole aim was to inculcate the three Rs in an effort to make children obedient and productive. The more advanced of our special schools have included as a key part of their regular teaching both social and community skills. Traditional curricula have included categories such as reading, writing, mathematics, language development, gross and fine motor skills, and so on. Modern curricula depend much more on the categories which are determined by the main areas of adult functioning such as caring for oneself, work, leisure, and participating in the local community. The more appropriately an individual behaves in the community the easier it is for integration to occur naturally. The teaching of such skills requires the dedicated patience of high quality teachers. Society must come to value the work of such teachers if progress towards integration is to be maintained and good teachers are to be attracted to, and maintained in, this specialised area.

The evaluation of quality of life has proved to be a complex area. Presumably the quality of life of people with a mental handicap will depend to a considerable extent on the success of the education system and, in reverse, a clear statement of those things which are taken to indicate a high quality of life should provide the basis for designing a successful school curriculum. Any measure of quality of life will depend upon the values that society holds. Wilcox and Bellamy (1982) propose that there are three dimensions which represent a synthesis of several contributions to this debate: productivity, independence and participation. Productivity is usually associated with paid employment and as well as providing an individual with access to many of life's pleasures, brings with it a way of structuring life, the feeling of being valued by others, the chance for personal growth and opportunities for social interaction. Although it is legitimate to question this value with its roots in the industrial society, it is clear that the majority of people still place high value on productive employment.

Most people choose a way of life which relies on other people for help and advice in certain areas of their life. In practice, however, forced dependence on others for help in achieving necessary daily activities is rarely valued. Education has already accepted that personal independence is an important goal. It has gradually become clear that such independence is not simply determined by an individual's skills but also by his or her ability to perform those skills *reliably*, by the absence of any problem behaviours and by the demands placed on the individual by the environment in which he or she lives. In the quest for this independence it is important that an individual's opportunities to progress towards living in an ordinary house in an ordinary community, with the advantages that flow from this, are not made dependent on first achieving such personal independence.

Finally, the dimension of participation is seen to imply access to all the facilities and opportunities that a particular community can offer. Most individuals choose for themselves the level at which they participate in the community, including social and leisure activities. People with a mental handicap have the right to similar choice and opportunities. Wilcox and Bellamy suggest that not only can these three factors provide a useful framework for evaluating the quality of life of an adult, but they can also be used as actual measures against which to define the outcomes for special education. There are, no doubt, many other values which could be used in a similar way, but these three are compatible with the desire for integration and provide a valuable starting point.

A strong body of opinion which has attempted to influence the way that services are provided for people with a mental handicap argues that service provision should follow the identification of each individual's role and *exact needs*. In practice, the nature of educational services has been largely determined by a variety of complex influences, including social, political, professional and economic factors. These factors were certainly largely responsible for the segregation of individuals into special education and will no doubt be important in the current moves to encourage integration (Barton and Tomlinson, 1984). The Education Act (1981) recognised that the categories used to label children's disabilities assumed that children had only one single disability. In practice no system of classification can take proper account of the variety of disabilities which can occur in any one child particularly when they are likely to change in time. The Act adopted the concept of 'special educational needs', as proposed in the Warnock Report, and recommended that the majority of these special needs could be met in ordinary schools 'as part of the integral provision that such schools make for the whole range of their pupils'. It was intended that the definition should include those needs which are attributable to 'a physical, sensory, or mental disability or an emotional or behavioural disorder and which call for special provision in respect of such matters as the location, content, timing or method of education'. Local Education Authorities (LEAs) are charged with the responsibility of reviewing and adjusting resources and their use so that pupils with special educational needs can be given the best opportunities to make progress. For children who cause the greatest concern to parents and teachers, a multi-professional assessment can be requested in which the medical, psychological and educational needs must be assessed by an appropriately qualified person. Any child who is officially 'recorded' as a result of such an assessment must have his special educational needs described and the LEA must state what steps it proposes to take to meet those needs.

On the important issue of integration the Act recognised that 'more and more people believe that, in order to give handicapped persons the same opportunities as other citizens, they should be involved in the ordinary processes of life and work to the maximum extent, and be integrated in their education with those who are not handicapped'. It was proposed that any child with special educational needs, whether that child was 'recorded' or not, should be educated with children who do not have such needs. This statement was made conditional on the efficient use of resources, the absence of any loss of efficiency in the education of the other children in the class or school, and the agreement of the child's parents. Special schools and a new category of independent schools were to be available for children who were 'recorded' who could not be integrated into ordinary education provision.

A recent review of the 1981 Education Act as it has been operated by the Derbyshire Local Education Authority (Kramer, 1985) has provided an interesting comment on the first 18 months of its operation. Parents reported that the recognition that their child had special needs was very upsetting and many felt guilt, shame, disbelief and a desire to blame either themselves or others. The majority of this 10 per cent sample of all those parents in Derbyshire whose child had been through the assessment and 'statementing' process felt that the service was good but there was dissatisfaction with certain features. Some parents felt that they had been unable to convince professionals of their real concerns about their child and they felt that the professionals had been slow to recognise some problems they had been raising for a long time. The assessment process was seen to be long-winded and the written reports were difficult to understand. What parents wanted most was immediate action to overcome the problems highlighted and this was linked to a concern over the level of resources available to meet special educational needs.

In the same article Kramer reported the views of staff working in mainstream schools on the integration issue. There was qualified support for integration but several conditions were seen as necessary for success. There was a need for appropriate advisory support which would be easily accessible. The administrative system would need to be sensitive and caring with an ability to respond to the unexpected. Staff would need to be well trained and sympathetic to the complex issues. Once again the need for more resources was stressed.

CONTINUING EDUCATION

If it is accepted that the goal of education is to equip people with the skills and knowledge to take part in work and social activities in society, then it is clear that education cannot stop at some pre-determined 'statutory' age. For people with a mental handicap the opportunity to continue with further or adult education of the appropriate sort can be extremely valuable. There have been many exciting developments in this area as innovative teachers and LEAs have made resources available to provide relevant courses and access to courses already attended by non-handicapped people. Colleges of Further Education have provided genuine opportunities for integration to occur both through specialised courses on topics such as social and life skills and through supporting individuals with a mental handicap to attend pre-vocational courses all run on the college campus. In some areas teachers who have for years provided education for people in segregated hospital schools have forged links with local further and adult education centres and are beginning to use such integrated settings for their work. There are many advantages to these developments, with students having opportunities to establish a more normal routine to their lives and experiencing a much wider range of natural events and interactions with non-handicapped peers. This educational process is two-way, and many of the fears and prejudices held by the general population should be gradually overcome.

A particularly exciting development is the increasing acceptance of the relevance of education and the skills of teachers to the world of real work. In one project in Sheffield several teachers have been released to work closely with other staff in setting up a small workshop designed to teach work skills to groups of between 8 and 15 severely handicapped individuals. Many of these individuals have previously been excluded from full-time education or occupation because of the severity of their handicap or a range of difficult or disruptive behaviour. After 18 months of operation in which simple skills have been taught using precision teaching methods and great patience, one such workshop has reduced the incidence of disruptive behaviour dramatically and is currently negotiating with a local firm for a contract to assemble a valued end-product for which the workers can be paid. This combination of teaching, psychological and manufacturing skills is a genuine breakthrough towards making education truly relevant.

REFERENCES

Barton, L. and Tomlinson, S. (1984). *Special Education and Social Interests*. Croom Helm, London.

Biklen, D. (1985). *Achieving the Complete School: Strategies for Effective Mainstreaming*. Teachers College Press, New York.

Burt, C. (1917). *The Distribution and Relations of Educational Abilities*. King and Son, London.

Donder, D. J. and York, R. (1984). In *Public School Integration of Severely Handicapped Students* (eds. Certo, N., Haring, N. and York, R.). Paul H. Brooks Publishing Co, Baltimore, USA.

Education Act 1981. HMSO, London.

Kramer, J. (1985). The 1981 Education Act in Derbyshire. *British Journal of Special Education*, **12**, 3, 98–101.

Stobart, M. (1984). Preparation for life – a Council of Europe project for the 1980s. *Journal of Community Education*, **3**, 1, 15–23.

Tomlinson, S. (1982). *A Sociology of Special Education*. Routledge and Kegan Paul, London.

Special Education Needs (the Warnock Report), Cmnd. 7212 (1978). HMSO, London.

Wilcox, B. and Bellamy, G. T. (1982). *Design of High School Programs for Severly Handicapped Students*. Paul H. Brooks Publishing Co, Baltimore, USA.

Wolfensberger, W. (1980). A brief overview of the principle of normalization. In *Normalization, Social Integration and Community Services* (eds. Flynn, J. R. and Nitsch, K. E.). University Park Press, Baltimore, USA.

Chapter 7

Work, Employment and Training

Being *disabled* does not mean *unable*

THE ROLE OF WORK IN PEOPLE'S LIVES

In recent years the Western world has started to think about what work means to the people who do it; it is usually necessary for an income, but that is not the whole story.

A generation of adults have reached retirement age since the war, with continuing better health and energy than their fore-bears enjoyed, so effort has been put into preparing them for a possible 20 future retired years, without employment but with satisfaction. It has long been recognised that life without one's job can be very depressing for men in particular, and prep-aration for retirement is now a serious undertaking. It started people thinking about the importance of work itself, of how people view themselves and each other.

Now that unemployment is so widespread, and in particular so many young adults of both sexes have never experienced regular employment, the effects have heightened society's in-terest in the nature of work, and what performing it does for people. We know for example that having no job to do leaves unemployed people without a sense of purpose, with no struc-ture to their days, with no drive to do anything else. People who are very slow to learn have also had no employment and experi-ence the same lack of purpose, structure and drive in life. Yet another social change has fuelled the debate about work: that is the shift in roles between the sexes, where most women are employed, in addition to doing traditional 'women's work', and many more men run homes for themselves and sometimes for their children, without the traditional 'woman's' input. This kind of work, however, is not often *paid* work. Indeed, looking at the total world population of adults one might say that half of it is occupied in feeding and cleaning the other half, in addition to themselves!

What then *is* work? Basically, it is the human attempt to control our environment: that is to acquire and retain food, warmth, clothing, shelter and to raise children.

In 'non-industrial' societies the whole family, which may include in-laws and cousins and grandparents, as an extended family, will share that work, children gathering fuel, caring for chickens and goats or minding the baby, with spinning and weaving performed in the home. All ages have a part in the work of survival and production. This was the situation in rural Britain, until the factories of the Industrial Revolution were built in the early nineteenth century, and people left the country for the growing towns, to work there. This was a different way of living: people worked in the employment of others, away from their own homes. We became the 'wage-based' society we live in now: instead of depending on ourselves to meet all our needs, we earn the money to spend on them.

There is a distinction to be made between work and paid employment. The same activity can be classed differently, according to the circumstances. A woman who visits and regularly supports her aged mother-in-law may have a heavy job on her hands, but that is not acknowledged as 'working', while a home help doing the same tasks receives both income and a valued status as such.

In our industrial society adults have been traditionally expected to 'go out to work', but also to ensure that the basic daily tasks of feeding, cleaning and sheltering are secured too, and the latter tasks have been traditionally assumed to be the responsibility of women. As noted earlier, these assumptions are being challenged now, particularly by younger adults. We all require a continuing investment of labour from somewhere for daily survival: to feed, dress, stay warm, clean and safe. Many of us take responsibility for it all, on our own behalf, or at least share it equitably. Others negotiate with housekeeping money or with salaries, for others to do it. But most slow learning adults have not been invited to provide on their own behalf that labour for daily maintenance. Thus a woman may devote her energies to dressing, catering for, cleaning, and occupying her adult daughter who has a mental handicap. She will not be paid for her hard work on her daughter's behalf; yet another person may perform the same tasks and be salaried as a care assistant. So often, however, such daughters and sons have reached adult life without having been taught to undertake personal responsibility for these tasks themselves. Some people have such severe disabilities that they remain in need of lots of support, but very many adults with a mental handicap have been left without an expectation of responsibility for themselves at all.

Children ordinarily grow up in the expectation of undertaking a share of the work involved in their own daily life: to learn to wash themselves, to contribute to the preparation and clearing of meals, to get themselves to school and back safely, and to occupy themselves at least some of the time. Preparation for the possible adult work roles starts very early in childhood with children identifying with adults of their own sex and developing expectations of following at least some of their examples. These will include the basic one of eventually being grown-up oneself ('and being able to do just as I like, and go to bed as late as I want, and being able to . . .'), of having one's own home, perhaps married, going out to work, having children. Having a working role (both in the domestic sense and in the employment sense) is built into the expectations of ordinary children, and becomes sharper at adolescence. The eventual effects of widespread unemployment on these youthful expectations are not yet known.

Work then, whether waged or unwaged, is necessary to provide the basic ingredients for survival. It does much more than that though: it puts a structure to our life, an organisation to daily existence which helps a sense of purpose. Employment affects how and where we live, the relationships we can have, what things we can buy, and what experiences we can undergo. (Can we afford a house, and where? Afford to have children? To travel abroad? Who shall we meet at work? Are our weekends free?)

In our Western society people are largely defined by how they are employed, and 'what they do'. Employment gives people an identity ('the new people next door, he's out of work but she's got a little cleaning job'). Although unemployed people may receive sympathy, people in employment have a better status, and the higher their earnings the more they can buy the attractive clothes, property and activities to improve their image and status still further. It is not only the material gains which enhance their image, however, it is the increased range of choices they can make in controlling their lives. Thus a disabled person with little income of his own and dependent on a poor parent has no choice of evening activity but to stay home: with an income they can choose to stay in or go out and pay for the means to do so.

WORK FOR PEOPLE WITH DISABILITIES

For many years there has been some public recognition that people with physical disabilities of all sorts need help in getting and performing jobs. Specialist charitable organisations have provided training and rehabilitation for open or sheltered employment for people with visual or mobility problems. The government runs employment rehabilitation centres (ERCs) throughout the UK, providing courses to help people who have been ill or disabled to return to employment. In promoting the employment of disabled people the Manpower Services

Commission (MSC) can arrange the free loan of physical aids, and fund modifications to premises and equipment if an employee's disability needs them, to enable work. He or she can have help with fares to work if severely disabled, and additional personal help may be available for blind people. Such forms of practical support make it possible for at least some people with big problems to function in the ordinary world of work alongside unhandicapped people.

There is a paradox in the fact that modern technology has both deprived people from many kinds of work, leaving them unemployed, yet at the same time enabled some people with severe disabilities to join in work they could not have done before. Thus, some people with cerebral palsy may operate electronic equipment both as disability aids and as tools (e.g. computers) of a job.

So far, though, the application of modern technology and training techniques to people with severe *intellectual* disabilities has been virtually ignored, with certain notable exceptions in the USA. The needs and rights of people with learning difficulties to be supported in unsegregated employment have simply not been considered, nor has there been clear thinking about their needs for training in personal survival skills. The traditional provision in the UK for half a century has been centres (initially set up by parents and volunteers) to provide occupation for mentally handicapped children and adults, which have evolved from occupation centres, to the adult training centres (ATCs) managed by social services departments and schools for children with severe learning difficulties run by departments of education. Anne's story illustrated how little preparation was available for real adult functioning in that system. Nevertheless there was an attempt to prepare some 'trainees' (labelled that even up to 60 years of age!) for open or sheltered employment, and contract work including sorting, packing, assembly and dismantling tasks have always been used. Any money made by ATCs in this way, however, belongs to the local authority, and the trainees gain none of it however well they work. While in that system, they are dependent on welfare benefits and can collect (in 1985) only £4 maximum weekly as reward money for their efforts: a reward understandably viewed with contempt by many trainees who await placement in employment. Meanwhile their labour is perceived and devalued as 'make-work'.

Less than 2 per cent of trainees in ATCs have moved on to sheltered or open industry in the last decade. It is important to remember that while 15–20 per cent of the general population in parts of Britain cannot find work, 98 per cent of people with intellectual disabilities have been unemployed, with all the damaging effects, for years.

ATCs and their forerunners were not primarily set up to meet the needs of the people with learning difficulties, but to provide families with relief during the day. Putting people with lots of problems together all the time is not a way to resolve them. As will be seen in the chapter on life in the institution, 'it serves other people's needs that they should live together, but not necessarily theirs' (Ryan and Thomas, 1980). During the past decade ATCs have had enormous pressures put on them. Until the mid-70s they catered for able-bodied trainees, capable of self-care, some of whom did move into employment. People with mobility, incontinence or behavioural problems were not candidates for ATCs: they either stayed at home with parents full time, or commonly became long-stay hospital residents. In 1970, however, an Education Act required even the most heavily handicapped of children to attend school. This piece of social policy, along with increasing short-term care, and improved teaching techniques, resulted in most severely intellectually disabled children remaining in the parental home into adult life: when schooling ended parents demanded a continuation of day placement and activities for their sons and daughters. In the late 1970s, therefore, ATCs were exhorted to provide facilities for people with severe and multiple handicaps; to offer much more education in number, literacy and daily living skills, and leisure opportunities. There is no question that these educational programmes are needed, but now it is asked, what are the appropriate settings?

ATCs (or social education centres) can be providing light industrial experience, cookery, literacy and money classes, outdoor leisure pursuits, and sessions with a speech or physiotherapist: all highly desirable but not normally provided in one's place of work. The characteristic way of 'total institutions' to blend all life's activities into one place is *not* how life is normally lived. Ordinary life requires some time and energy spent on survival and comfort needs, some of it for earning money, and some for leisure pursuits. If employment requires skill training, it is usually provided as part of the job. Learning about cookery, car maintenance or computers if it is unrelated to employment, is acquired in adult education, away from work, and similarly separate settings apply for leisure and sports activities. In the world of real work, employers provide such training as they require for unskilled and semi-skilled jobs, on the shop floor. People with learning difficulties benefit from learning new skills and practising them, in the very place they need to apply them. In other words, why teach skills in 'pretend' accommodation, instead of the workshop or kitchen they will be occupying daily in the future? Because of insufficient preparation earlier in life, there may be inadequacies in how the disabled person functions socially in a workplace. What better models of ordinary conduct to copy are there, than the other ordinary workers? To enable an individual with learning difficulties to work in such open or sheltered employment is likely to require the presence of another person for support and counselling at least initially. There are already ways by which such supporters can be funded, but current bureaucratic delays can be a disincentive to willing employers.

People with intellectual disabilities usually grow up with little experience of making choices or taking decisions; somebody else, or society at large, makes the decisions for them. In Anne's story, the ATC staff and her parents decided for her that she should not have a sexual relationship and that she should leave her social world of the centre and stay at home in her parents' house. Even in adult life her clothes were still chosen for her. To have a job in the world of real work provides a confirmation of adult status and income, and mentally handicapped people have a right to experience jobs from which to learn to choose.

There has always been a major assumption in providing services for people with an intellectual disability, that is, they have been expected to climb up various ladders of progress to prove to society that they are worthy to live domestic lives or to share the world of work like other citizens do. For those very slow learners who have found themselves pigeonholed with segregated labels and placements, the way back out of a segregated life has been almost impossible. The right to be *supported* in ordinary employment is already acknowledged for physical disability and it exists no less for people with intellectual disability. The question to be asked is not 'Could s/he do that job unaided?' but 'What *support* would s/he need to do the job alongside non-handicapped people?' There is now an expanding body of experience in job finding and holding by people with mental handicaps, aided by various professionals employed as job finders, interested employers, and supportive workmates and 'foster workers'. Further information on such employment possibilities is provided at the end of the book. It will take a variety of initiatives and approaches to make real work accessible to all the intellectually disabled people in the years to come.

There are thousands of adults between the ages of 19 and 60 in ATCs, being trained and supported by instructors with a wide range of work and social skills. The wealth of experience at present held within the walls of ATCs can be shared and applied in a wide range of working experiences, ordinary job support and training situations in the outside world, and many ATCs are already re-deploying staff to support their clients as real employees in unsegregated settings. Clients who have encountered adult life only in the ATC need support while they gain confidence and social skills in their new workplace. So, of course, do their parents for whom the image of their son or daughter as a responsible wage earner may be a difficult one to accept at first.

Young people leaving special schools hold few expectations of work for themselves; neither do their parents or their teachers. The future expectations for them are usually the ATC for 40 years, celibacy and being life-long guests in their parents' home. The British educational system now promotes integration of children with disabilities in ordinary schools, and children who are very slow learners will have more opportunity in the future to encounter ordinary life expectations. There are already systems whereby young people can participate in work experience of all varieties, there are courses in local colleges of further education serving people of all intellectual abilities; what is required is a quite fresh approach to the needs and entitlements of young adults who happen to be very slow learners but who have at least 40 years in which to use the ordinary skills of work and life in an ordinary life setting. It is common for intellectually disabled young people to leave school still lacking a number of skills in 'personal survival', road or transport use, personal care, or recognising normal adult courtesies and customs. Their problems can possibly include incontinence. All these deficits may be seen as barriers to work placement and their remediation seen as the first target before employment. For many such young people, personal support in a normal adult environment away from 'handicapped expectations' encourages them in efforts to learn how to use buses, and to behave maturely. Incontinence is a major nuisance: it can arise from a range of causes and needs careful diagnosis followed by appropriate management. However, when considering the additional physical problems which some intellectually disabled people have, such as epilepsy or spasticity or deafness or incontinence, it is essential to examine their problem as though the individual is not mentally handicapped. There are thousands of people of all ages in the population not intellectually disabled who have mobility problems or who are incontinent or have fits. Their problems may be helped by medication and appliances and environmental manipulation. The same approach of isolating the specific problem and applying modern resources to it is just as necessary for people who in addition happen to be very slow learners.

For some intellectually disabled people a major difficulty is learning how to sustain attention in any one activity or interest. Some children and young people will demonstrate this by their restlessness and demands for personal interaction; it can be exhaustingly disruptive. Others may apply their energy to rocking, head banging, or other assaults on themselves or other people. Long-standing practices like these have understandably been seen as hopeless barriers to real work. Disruptive and anti-social behaviour are massive handicaps which lead to all sorts of secondary problems and deprivations. These forms of handicap demand the most thorough attention to its management.

Work pioneered in the United States for over 10 years has demonstrated that the problem of severe disruptive behaviour can be tackled in a different and productive way. Bellamy and others (1979) have established a network of commercial business in electronics across America, which employs severely intellectually disabled people, including those with major behavioural problems, on a fully commercial basis. Certain basic practices underlie the successes of this special training programme (STP). First, there is the recognition that if any undesirable behaviour (e.g. rocking, hitting, etc.) is to be stopped then some other desirable activity must be identified to replace it. In the workshop that means activities appropriate in that work-setting. Then positive rewards which have meaning for the individual must also be identified and available when the desired behaviours occur. The whole environment is manipulated to encourage the new work activities and to make unwanted behaviours difficult or unrewarding. The second practice is that known as precision teaching. This means breaking down the tasks into very, very small steps and teaching each one with a reward where necessary. The activities involved in mastering a skill are all the ones with which to replace disruptive behaviour. For some institutionalised clients, the first steps on the road to paid employment as an assembly worker in the micro-tech industry can be having to *learn to sit at a bench for a few minutes*, without wandering off, and simply looking at an object before picking it up and putting it in a specified place. This, of course, requires intensive staff supervision and suitable reward for every stage achieved. The rewards are reduced and spaced out or changed as progress is made. The satisfaction of completing a task is the ordinary human reward which slow learners are helped to experience too. At the beginning of such training the employee is fairly costly to support, but after about two years the trained workers are earning proper wages and the workshops are commercial concerns. Two years is not an unreasonable investment for a future lifetime of productive employment, respected worker status and a real income.

There is in the UK, after the school leavers and the adults in ATCs, a third group of people with intellectual disabilities and special difficulties. They are the individuals who have spent many years of their lives away from ordinary social existence living in mental handicap hospitals. Often their problems are multiple and there were no solutions available at their time of admission. Real adult work has not existed for them: their activities have been 'make-work', diversions, occupations, timefillers or nothing. The ordinary disciplines, satisfactions and rewards of real work have remained unknown to them. This applies not only to paid employment but to the whole area of (usually unpaid) work concerned with the maintenance of living: preparing meals, cleaning and keeping control over home and person. The maintenance of life is managed by the hospital. When hospital residents move out into community living, learning slowly those household functions taken for granted by most of us can occupy large and very enjoyable portions of their day.

We all need purpose in life and our mental health is promoted by occupations which control our environment and provide social interaction and self-respect. People with learning difficulties or any other disabilities are part of our human society, with no less need for valued occupations, but rather more need for support to perform them.

REFERENCES

Bellamy, G. T., Horner, R. H. and Inman, D. P. (1979). *Vocational Habilitation of Severely Retarded Adults*. University Park Press, Baltimore, USA.

Ryan, J. and Thomas, F. (1980). *The Politics of Mental Handicap*. Penguin Books, Harmondsworth.

FURTHER READING

King's Fund Centre (1984). *An Ordinary Working Life: Vocational Services for People with Mental Handicap*. King's Fund Project Paper No. 50, London.

Chapter 8

Recreation and Leisure Opportunities

Most of our lives are broken down into two active sessions, work and leisure. In this chapter we look at the very positive advantages of making available opportunities to all mentally handicapped people by the development of recreational and leisure activities. Like all of us, mentally handicapped people are individuals and what suits some in terms of recreation may not suit others. We develop our social/recreational skills and preferences by a system of trial and error. From early childhood we experiment with various hobbies, games, clubs, etc. In following all these pursuits we acquire many spin-off skills such as team spirit, concentration, physical activity, the skills of balance, hearing, and so on. There are two major factors of importance in reaching our final decisions on what sort of hobbies or sports to pursue, namely opportunity and choice. Many mentally handicapped people for a variety of reasons have a history of limited choice. In this chapter examples are given that may encourage you to experiment with alternatives for mentally handicapped people that may in turn develop a new hobby or pursuit for yourself.

INFLUENCING FACTORS

Throughout this book reference is made to developmental opportunities. That principle is particularly important in this chapter. Many handicapped people have limited opportunities because it is thought that they will be unable to participate and won't enjoy the experience. The idea that mentally handicapped people are really just children has tended to lead to restricted opportunities for them. An example of such thinking is found in the amount of playgrounds found in services for adults who are mentally handicapped. While many residents would enjoy such places often such activities do not help them to be seen as dignified or adult. Because we have tended to restrict the opportunities, when they are expanded they are often eagerly pursued. Wherever possible, mentally handicapped people should enjoy their leisure activities alongside other members of society. This practice helps social integration and does not restrict them to special opportunities, which are often limited. Obviously there will be exceptions where, because of the degree of handicap or lack of suitable facilities, this is not possible, but such restrictions are few.

RISK TAKING

Historically, concern for the physical well-being of handicapped people has tended to restrict many opportunities. A good example is the person suffering from epilepsy who may wish to pursue swimming – while there is a risk in such an activity it can, in reality, be minimal but could be grossly overemphasised. If all safety precautions are strictly observed, then the risk factor can be reduced to a suitable level. Taking no risks in life tends grossly to restrict opportunities and disabled peoples' potential lives then get wrapped in cotton wool – this is a situation which we would not accept for ourselves but is one that can easily be imposed on handicapped people. Sports considered high risk, such as pot-holing or rock climbing, are now standard pursuits at most outward-bound courses for mentally handicapped people who are in good health. Well trained and experienced instructors are the obvious keys to a successful and reduced risk adventure. While we may not relish the thought of such an experience ourselves many mentally handicapped do. Risk is reduced if the same guidelines that normal people would follow are applied, such as start slow, take regular exercise, have a good diet, etc. On the whole, the risks to disabled people are no more than to ourselves, with one or two exceptions. Some handicapped people may have heart conditions which need special attention and abnormalities of the bones such as in Down's syndrome where exercises which involve trampolining or jumping up and down are not always advisable. Any anxieties that might exist could be easily eliminated by seeking medical advice before becoming involved in the event.

CHOICES

In this section some practical ideas for developing recreation/ leisure activities are put forward under broad headings with a few specific examples in detail.

Sports

Over the past few years there has been a gradual increase and development of leisure centres in this country. Nearly all such centres have an extensive range of indoor sports. Most large towns and cities have several sports complexes; in addition many schools now open and allow access by the public to their indoor facilities such as gymnasia halls and swimming pools as well as their outdoor facilities.

SWIMMING

Swimming as a sport in the United Kingdom is high on the list of activities. A number of hospitals and training centres now actively participate in such schemes, many sponsored by the Amateur Swimming Association. Apart from the ability of the physically mobile to learn to swim which, in turn, gives them extra confidence and self-reliance, there is the spin-off factor that being able to swim opens up other opportunities such as canoeing and sailing. It is obviously much easier to teach children to swim than adults, if only because of their size. Even the most profoundly handicapped person gains from this activity: the actual weightlessness of the body is found to be extremely therapeutic. The use of inflatable equipment such as armbands and rings helps maintain buoyancy and through exposure to experience confidence is gained. It is important that anyone supervising activities in the water must be suitably qualified. Apart from learning to swim, people can also take part in pool games. Many handicapped people have acquired certificates for swimming once the opportunity was made available to them.

BALL GAMES

Ball games can be played either indoors or outdoors. They can be played in a one-to-one situation or as a team or group. Simple stages – such as bouncing, passing, throwing, rolling – once acquired, allow other opportunities to develop. The throwing and catching of a ball helps develop the hand/eye coordination required for other ball games. We have seen examples of wheelchair basketball and wheelchair polo where some mastery of ball control is required. For the more ablebodied, games such as football and basketball not only encourage and develop the individual as an individual but also as part of a team. Not all activity needs to be energetic; once the basic skill of handling the ball has been taught, other games such as bowling, croquet or table skittles then become possible.

Hobbies

In this section we suggest things of particular interest to the individual yet not necessarily things to be done alone. The items in this section are endless and perhaps are not quite so energetic as in sports.

MUSIC

Many mentally handicapped people are exposed to music daily and many take great enjoyment in listening to it. In terms of a hobby it may be simply the opportunity to possess a personal tape-recorder with a set of headphones or a music centre with records. Opportunities for handicapped people to go and listen to live music are rare, although as more facilities for handicapped people develop so they should increase. Quite often one sees music workshops where people are given the opportunity to go along and strum a guitar or bang a drum. The sensations of that are pleasing not only for handicapped people but for ourselves. Music, in turn, teaches rhythm and sound variation.

COLLECTING

Many handicapped people, like ourselves, are very proud of the possessions that they have collected during their life. While the items they collect may be of little value, to the individual they are of great importance. Indeed, they may seem odd to ourselves but are nevertheless of great emotional value. Such items collected can range from bottle tops to records, dolls to coins to stamps – the list is endless. Whatever is of value to the individual is what is important.

WALKING

While giving people the opportunity of exercise, walking also opens up other learning opportunities. Walking either in town or country gives us all the chance to observe life and understand our world.

FISHING

This popular pastime again takes advantage of the outdoors. The major requirements apart from tackle are patience and a degree of hand/eye co-ordination, but while sitting waiting for the fish we have opportunities to observe wildlife and to use the whole experience to broaden our life.

DANCING

This pastime/hobby can include all types of dance from ball-room to country. In country dancing a degree of rhythm and co-ordination is required and this too can be developed as part of a team. The opportunities to visit many places to dance also opens new horizons.

GARDENING

Many handicapped people either at school or training centres participate in gardening. The skills of hand/eye co-ordination are required for planting out seeds and seedlings. The need to water and tend the plants is of some interest, but the major reward is actually the growing of a flower or plant. This type of activity is possible virtually regardless of handicap and the rewards for effort are always pleasing.

'Spectating'

As we consider this, many examples come to mind including films, football, car racing, horse racing. Many clubs provide on-site facilities for watching, such as club houses. If choice is to be afforded for the handicapped then facilities must be provided of a suitable nature.

Holidays

For many years, holidays for handicapped people presented problems, but companies are now much more receptive to the needs of the disabled with some actually gearing their services for such groups. The provision of specially-adapted facilities and simple changes such as ramps have opened up many possibilities for the physically disabled person.

CAMPING

Most people at some point in their lives have been camping.

There is no doubt that the experience of living under canvas in the country is quite different from any other experience. On a camping holiday many new experiences, such as cooking and making one's bed, are challenges that enable new skills to be developed. We know of many handicapped people who have benefited greatly from these activities and would advocate such holidays as a major change from daily life.

HOLIDAYS ABROAD

While there are many varied and beautiful holidays available in this country, a holiday abroad requires a new type of thinking. For anyone the first experience is both a challenge and a great adventure. From our own experiences the delight of flying and of sailing produced new dimensions to our lives. The opportunity to sample different foods, language and climate all add to appreciation of alternatives. In recent years the authors have seen many holidays offered for handicapped people to visit a variety of countries – one rated very highly is North America where the variation of experience can be extremely beneficial.

ADVENTURE HOLIDAYS

Outward bound holidays are now available to disabled people, including canoeing, sailing, pot-holing and pony trekking. All these activities are designed to develop the individual in terms of experience and self-reliance; such holidays are very closely supervised with well trained instructors and are highly beneficial.

Guides and Scouts

Many physically and mentally handicapped people belong to either the Scouts or Guides organisations. The opportunities afforded by such groups are countless, ranging from camping holidays to the club-like atmosphere of weekly meetings. Their emphasis on skill-learning is beneficial to their mental handicap members.

Adult Education

For the average person the services provided by adult education classes have grown considerably over recent years. Mentally handicapped people now attend adult education classes and participate in living-skill development systems. The authors know many who attend adult literacy classes, cookery, woodwork, etc. Among the opportunities offered by the local authority, the adult education system is one area that should be explored by everyone.

There are numerous books and pamphlets available as well as videos which give examples of leisure activities and opportunities that are available for the handicapped. Special insurance may be required for some holidays abroad and certain activities; advice should be sought from a reputable insurance broker.

A dilemma faced by ageing parents is that of having a child who might wish to participate in some of these programmes while they themselves may not. Many facilities are available via the local authority and for parents who may not wish to participate themselves, there are helpers, employed by the local authority or through voluntary groups, available to assist handicapped people undertake some of these experiences. The local authority or a voluntary organisation such as MENCAP can give advice.

All these activities and many others are available but they should be geared to the wishes of the individual. Before decisions can be made as to which are the most enjoyable and beneficial the opportunity to try them must be made available. The development of leisure pursuits can open up a whole new life for disabled people and should be as available to them as to ourselves.

USEFUL BOOKS

Alvin, J. (1976). *Music for the Handicapped Child*. Oxford University Press, Oxford.

Association of Swimming Therapy. *Swimming for the Disabled*. A & C Black, London.

Atack, S. M. (1980). *Art Activities for the Handicapped*. Souvenir Press, London.

Baum, L. *Stimulation through Play*. MENCAP, London.

Cotton, M. (1981). *Out of Doors with Handicapped People*. Souvenir Press, London.

Cotton, M. (1983). *Outdoor Adventure for Handicapped People*. Souvenir Press, London.

Evans, D. R. *Dried Flowers: Horticulture for the Mentally Handicapped*. University of Bath, Bath.

Hart, G. J. and Edwards, A.T.S. *Wheelchair Dances*: Book 2 (1976); Book 3 (1980). Spastics Society, London.

Latto, K. (1981). *Give us a Chance: Sport and Physical Recreation with Mentally Handicapped People*. Disabled Living Foundation, London.

Marshall, R. M. (1983). *My Cook Book*. British Institute of Mental Handicap, Kidderminster.

Way, B. (1967). *Development through Drama*. Longmans, London.

Wood, M. (1985). *Music for Mentally Handicapped People*. Souvenir Press, London.

Chapter 9
Residential Needs

It has become more and more obvious over the past few years that the most positive environment for mentally handicapped people to live in is their parental home. Services provided to help maintain and support such people in that setting have grown and developed considerably. Much earlier this century the majority of advice given to parents was to have them 'put away'. It was considered the kindest thing to do, for it would thus provide for the child everything required such as warmth, food, etc. It would free the family from the burden of care and would allow them to 'try again'. It was suggested that this was the kindest thing for handicapped children as nothing could be done for them. This approach has resulted in mentally handicapped people being congregated together in large numbers often in isolated places.

While many parents took this advice as it was considered 'right and proper' many suffered considerable anguish and guilt, and some still do. Fortunately, this opinion is now no longer considered appropriate by professionals involved in providing services, although the view still exists in society today – mainly through ignorance.

Sadly, even today we see examples, though somewhat watered down, of that same attitude from organisations directly involved. You may still see mentally handicapped people being 'advertised' in an appeal on TV or on collection boxes as being in need of specialised care, which still has the same congregational/isolationist role. This does not help the social image of intellectually disabled people, nor does it help to establish them as dignified members of our society, but merely people who require sympathy and care.

Perhaps because they were seen as 'children' throughout their lives it helped, but statutory right as opposed to well-meaning charity is always more acceptable. Parents who kept their children at home always had to live with the anxiety of what would happen when they died or could no longer cope. Many families have saved throughout their lives in order to amass what might be an amount sufficient to provide for private care. For many families these life savings are grossly insufficient. Private care can be extremely expensive, even that provided by charities, and sums of £200 per week are not unknown.

THE PRESENT SITUATION

Health

Many of our present-day mental handicap services are still based within what were originally workhouses. Even some of the present developments of services for mentally handicapped people have continued the practice of segregation and congregation.

Continuing segregation/congregation system

It was (and still is) difficult enough for society to accept that such groups of people exist. The need to remove them from the eyes of society has resulted in the development of services in institutions usually built in the country and surrounded with high walls. A place to be feared and a place where all the negative social values could be concentrated. The average person in society knew of their existence but did not need to worry as the danger of being tainted was extremely limited. It created a social distance which was the expectation of that society. Unfortunately, the social distancing has been reinforced by the myths of the institution and the events that go on behind the walls. Only in the last 20 years have we really seen any major change towards an openness and honesty about what does go on within the institutional system.

The medical model

Regrettably for the mentally handicapped, being linked with other groups of people considered in need of care has reinforced society's negative views of them. Perhaps the best example is the linking and continuous misunderstanding of the difference between 'mental illness' and 'mental handicap' – this is not only within society at large but within organisations actually involved in providing services for the mentally ill and mentally handicapped. The two are poles apart and yet, because of their similar administrative structure and the view of the way in which to 'treat' these people, confusion continues to exist and in some cases be reinforced. The major reason for this development lies within the structure of the organisation which deemed or was deemed to have the necessary skills to provide services, namely doctors and the NHS.

The emergence of treatment for mental illness was seen in the 1950s, and of the developmental change that took place within the psychiatric services there is no doubt. The revolution that was brought about, particularly by the introduction of phenothiazines (major tranquillisers), changed the world of the psychiatric institution. Unfortunately, the same model of providing services was bestowed on mentally handicapped people as well – but drugs do not cure mental handicap. What one has within the medical model is the scientific type view. In reality, being linked with that scientific approach and the mystique of medicine the result for mentally handicapped people is extremely negative. If one takes the mental handicap population of this country as a whole, then their medical needs are really no different from yours and mine. Equally their nursing needs are no different. They are trapped within a social view that mental handicap is a disease process and, therefore, to some extent curable. This is just not so. Improvements in the skill and ability of mentally handicapped people can be made but they are not brought about by the world of medicine. We have argued the point throughout that mental handicap is a social and educational dilemma.

The NHS, because of its historical linking (and for no other reason), is now providing residential services for the intellectually disabled. It is obviously a very positive approach and there is no doubt that considerable efforts are taking place within that model. Unfortunately, the ability of the NHS and the medical and allied professions to provide appropriate developmental services are considerably reduced. Statutory training of professionals who work within that model have, until recently, been truly medically orientated. It is, of course, important that within our society we have the medical and genetic knowledge in order to aid prevention or to minimise the possible physical and psychological effect of being handicapped but the need to provide services still requires a more appropriate approach. How can anyone be expected to provide such a service in a system which deprives them of opportunities for growth in a totally false environment?

The social model

This has developed impetus over the past 20 years with the assistance and development of education and social services for mentally handicapped people, the emergence of charities and a more normal and supportive approach to caring for handicapped people within our society.

Many handicapped people no longer walk the path that leads them to a lifetime of institutional care. If one is going to attempt to identify what are the residential needs for handicapped people, then perhaps we need only look to ourselves and ask for what we should wish. Prior to that, is it worth looking at what services have developed in the last few years and the first attempts to provide for consumer needs and not merely to accept the continuation of the past? It is also regrettable to note that while in Britain at this time we have a policy of community care, many opportunities are being lost. Many large hospitals are being run down and their former residents discharged. Some authorities attempt to re-locate them in a personalised and sensitive manner, others do not.

Many authorities faced with the need to find alternatives are looking for 'off the shelf' models. Advice in the form of: If you have a total population of X you need Y beds. The answer is Z hostels and small hospitals. It is not only an expensive approach – cost of building, maintenance, gas, electricity, cooking – but it also reinforces a model that congregates people. It often results in public debate and opposition and in the longer term does nothing to help mentally handicapped people live anything like an ordinary life. Residential services should be available for both the short-term and the long-term.

SERVICES AVAILABLE TODAY

Short-term care services

One of the major reasons why people who are disabled require residential short-care services is because the primary care-giver is temporarily unable to provide care, for whatever reason. The problem is what alternatives are available, the demand for those places and what those services will actually provide. This is still a major concern for any parent of a disabled person, because she may need relief from the stress of caring from time to time. One of the methods employed by various organisations, particularly the health and local authority social services departments, has been to provide short-term care. These respite services are mainly for the primary care-giver to allow her to take a break. Unfortunately many get caught in the 'double bind' in that they book months in advance, because they are concerned not to lose their booking to someone else and so not get the respite that they so desperately need.

The other concern in developing short-term care services is that when the primary care-giver is no longer able to cope the handicapped person will be able to enter the same environment on a longer-term basis. This raises many questions concerning the management of services because this goal means that the original placement must be very carefully selected.

Certainly the advantage in the provision of short-term care services has meant that many mentally handicapped people have stayed at home and within society much longer. It is not uncommon for many elderly, often single-parent, families to go on using this help over a long period and in our experience there are many people in this position. A new dilemma now exists. Over the next 15 years the demand for long-term care will increase considerably. Without positive planning a major problem faces providers in the next two decades. With present 'community care' policies few of the older refuges will be available in the NHS and the local authority will be faced with major difficulties in providing care. The development of short-term care services along with day-care services has relieved considerably the burden on families who care for their offspring. It has also allowed those people to develop their individual lives instead of having to provide 24-hour services on their own. The disadvantage is obvious for the handicapped: there is the disruption this creates for the handicapped person in his normal flow of life, and the potential abnormality of the setting that receives him. There are several ways in which some of the issues may be resolved. These difficulties and some possible answers are covered later.

Long-term residential services – a place to live

At some point in the life of the intellectually disabled person some long-term home will be required, either in childhood, adolescence or in mid-life when the primary care-giver is no longer able to cope. If the disabled person has been used to having his lifestyle changed, then such a move may not present major difficulties but, for those who have always been at home, the trauma of sudden departure can be extremely disturbing for both the individual and his family. Anxiety as the primary carers get older causes growing and tremendous distress. They feel no one else could replace the personal elements they have provided, probably since birth, and they are right, but sensitive services can provide a positive and meaningful life.

Unlike the average family where the expectation of the parents is responsibility for the child from birth until independence, which is usually demonstrated by their child moving on or marrying, the mentally handicapped child is likely to remain at home. For some parents this is a very positive and rewarding situation, but for the handicapped person who has been at home all his life and who suddenly at the age of 40 must leave and start again it can create major trauma. To start to develop all the interactions and knowledge they will require to make their future life more acceptable is extremely complex and difficult. Fortunately such examples are becoming less common.

The requirements of statutory authorities such as education help to prepare the growing disabled person: they go to school, they form friendships and they are open to many experiences that make the eventual trauma of leaving the parental home easier. It is still a fact that in the UK the majority of residential services for the intellectually disabled are still unsatisfactory. The major reason for this is cost. The economy of scale argues that the more people you get into the space under one roof the cheaper it will be. It is cheaper to cook for 50 than for 1 or 2. There is a danger that with the best intentions an organisation will still have to resort to warehousing – where the handicapped person is one of many where congregation and segregation are reinforced and perpetuated. There is actually no reason why this need be so, but it does require a far more imaginative use of resources and a greater amount of money and time in order to stop such a system being perpetuated.

WHAT SHOULD RESIDENTIAL SERVICES PROVIDE? FUTURE POSSIBILITIES

In order to consider this we need to look at short-term and long-term services slightly differently.

Short-term services should consider just that, long-term services should consider the provision of a home; but there are common denominators. Both should provide shelter and care. They should promote independence and treat the individual with understanding and dignity. Services will be appropriate to need only if based on individuals and not groups and if they fit into some flexible pattern. It is also important that it be as local as possible.

Short-term provision

This is usually the starting point for families who are releasing their offspring into the wider world. It is this resource that will help support the family until a longer-term solution is required. It would be unfair to mix long- and short-term residential provisions mainly because the needs of the two groups vary so much. Long-term provision is the provision of a home; those using short-term care services already live at home. Services should be concentrated so that the individual is not confused. The provision of a key-worker (community support worker) can help liaison between the agency and the family. A partnership based on an agreed, shared workload is imperative if the handicapped person is to derive the maximum benefit from the experience. If the brother or sister of the handicapped person was going away for the weekend with the Brownies, Guides, Cubs or Scouts the parents would be pleased because the benefits would be new experience and personal development. For the mentally handicapped this is how short-term care systems should work – based on the developmental needs identified and agreed in an individual programme and these should be continued consistently. It is important that such events are as positive as possible for both the handicapped person and the family as they will reinforce and support long-term community living.

To minimise trauma small locally-based services must be provided. The handicapped person will be used to living in an ordinary house and, therefore, it is logical that short-term care should be provided in a similar place. Large institutions with sitting rooms for 20–30 people present a completely different world, and a frightening one. It is the reverse of the situation faced in a de-institutionalisation programme when, after years of mass living, people are made anxious by lowered noise level, lack of institutional programming and congregation. If we were using such a 'small' system, we should possibly visualise the following:

A FACE I KNOW

If there was someone there I knew and who knew me, I might feel reassured and secure, perhaps a staff member who would act as a link between my day-to-day life and this part of my life – he might be called my key-worker, someone who knows and perhaps understands me, someone who would take a little extra interest in me and the rest of my family. He would try and understand what I like or dislike – what jobs I could do – perhaps teach me to do more things for myself, which would be helpful to me and my family. My key-worker might do many things for me but would always help me make the best of any experience.

THE TEMPORARY HOME

It should have a feeling of homeliness and give me a feeling of belonging. It should provide me with learning opportunities because one day I shall probably have to move into a home like this. It should be 'normal', not full of locked rooms, shared bedrooms and staff in uniforms. It should be 'safe' enough to meet my needs, but I shouldn't be living with people who have special needs over and above mine, forcing me to live in a restrictive environment. It could and should provide me with basic requirements such as food (food I like), and other things of importance and value to me.

THINGS TO DO

During my stay we should do things – I don't want to sit doing nothing from breakfast to lunch, lunch to dinner, dinner to bed, and for that to be repeated tomorrow. If after breakfast I usually go to school or work, then I should go out and return here at night. Some nights we should go out, but not necessarily every night. If we go out we don't always have to go with other handicapped people – we could do something different. There isn't a law against it.

Although these comments will seem pretty obvious to the reader, the reality isn't always so.

Resolving the 'double bind'

In the previous section the issue of long-term thinking was related to short-term services and the difficulties that this presents. The first is the problem of inadequate resources which means that you must book continuously so as not to lose your place. Investing in short-term residential services is in the long term very cost-efficient. One bed plus support services can provide 52 weeks of respite per year. That is a service for 52 primary care-givers at 1 week per family. As one would not wish to see a warehousing system, no more than approximately 3 beds should be considered, providing 156 families with respite.

The other problem is whether a short-term place should become a long-term place. We feel it should not. It would severely restrict the ebb and flow of the short-term place, and severely disrupt the lifestyles of permanent residents. Compatibility of individuals in long-term systems is very important and such temporary intrusion is unsatisfactory. Short-term care systems should work towards compatibility and forecasting possible long-term residents.

Long-term residential needs

Over the past 20 years, with increasing awareness and improved services, parents of handicapped children have attempted to keep their children in the family home. The development of short-term respite services has played a very important part in supporting this. For many parents this has been an anxiety-provoking experience, but many have resolved the conflict. Their anxieties about safety and welfare have been resolved and most families have learned to value such services.

This still leaves parents concerned for the future. Should we keep him at home until we die? Should we let him go now? But go where? Should it be so final? The decision is perhaps the most difficult one the family has to face, but face it they must. Services need not be so black and white and the personalising of care systems is the only possible answer.

Many of the elements that make up short-term services are equally applicable to providing handicapped people with a long-term home, but it is worth repeating key points: stability, companionship, friendship, counsel, support, opportunities to grow and develop, an environment where handicapped people are valued and treated as equals. The most helpful factor for the handicapped person is to be one of few rather than many, so that advantage may be taken of developmental experiences. The first possible choice is his own home, supported by staff. It could be the parental home or the home of a relative. If this is not possible, then someone else's home. The development of long-term fostering-type arrangements for intellectually disabled adults is one that is now receiving extensive support.

Many couples whose children have grown up and left the family home are offering long-term services to intellectually disabled individuals. Some of these families have worked with disabled people for many years or have been foster parents throughout their lives. There are critics of this scheme but if it is well supported and externally monitored the quality of the service is exceptional and rewarding to both parties.

Many handicapped people who have been in institutional services for many years have inherited or accumulated large sums of money and are able to purchase property of their own, or, if long-standing relationships exist, they could be co-owners of property. Tenancy of council property either alone or with others is another alternative. All of these solutions offer the mentally handicapped individual the recognition that he (or she) requires the same opportunities as the rest of us and should not be in a system that depersonalises.

Support staffing

The other vital element worthy of further consideration is that of support staff. It would be unrealistic to abandon mentally handicapped people in their own homes without giving them some means by which they can be represented.

Not to recognise that handicapped people are different would be not only unrealistic but also discreditable. A system allowing handicapped people to walk the streets aimlessly is unacceptable, but the authors maintain that they must be allowed to live lives that are the least restrictive, receive services that are the least intrusive and that are sensitive in recognising and facilitating developmental opportunities.

All staff working with intellectually disabled people must be able to embrace these principles and apply them to their day-to-day encounters in a positive and respectful way if such people are to enjoy and understand the meaning of an ordinary life.

Apart from these normative needs, the intellectually disabled should use all normal resources and the degree of support should be tailored to their needs, recognising that needs do change. If such blueprints become reality then perhaps mentally handicapped people may have a reasonable quality of life.

Chapter 10

Life in an Institution and Beyond

INTRODUCTION

Throughout history people have grouped themselves together to share activities either voluntarily, or under differing degrees of social compulsion. Hunting tribes, Greek armies, Roman senators, medieval monasteries, ships, prisons, schools, hospitals and factories, are varieties of social establishments where people have assembled for some common purpose. These social establishments are all 'institutions': some, such as a public market, are open for almost anybody to enter and leave; some clubs may be very selective, and prison is an unpopular variety imposed on offenders by society.

In everyday life human activities break down into sleep, work and play; in Western society they occur usually with different people, in different settings, and under different 'rules'. One's activities, companions and responsibilities vary, for example, in the school or factory, the home, and the sports centre or pub, although there may be some slight overlap. We move from one setting and activity to another, directed by a mixture of social pressures and personal choices. Most of the settings are themselves varieties of institutions, the 'authority' in each compartment of life is limited usually to just that part: for example, the factory foreman has no responsibility to decide his workers' choice of Sunday visitors at home, nor does the swimming coach expect to have any say in how the workers

dresses in the home or factory. But there are some social establishments where these barriers between sections of life have
been removed, where all aspects of life are conducted in the
same place and under the same authority, in the constant company of a lot of other people who are all treated alike and are all
expected to perform together. These establishments are known
as 'total institutions' and while Erving Goffman (1961) in his
classic book *Asylums* describes their activities with special reference to psychiatric hospitals, he also illustrates them with
examples from army life, boarding schools and prisons. That
book should be read by all who work in the care or supervision
of other people and much of this chapter is based on its observations.

Goffman describes five kinds of total institution:

1. for people who are incapable and harmless, such as orphan-
   ages and old people's homes

2. for incapable people but those who may present a threat to
   the community, even if unintentionally, such as lepers,
   psychiatrically ill and mentally handicapped people.

3. institutions to protect the public from deliberate harm, that
   is prisons, in which the well-being of the inmates is the
   secondary concern

4. institutions devoted to achieving a work-like task, for
   example army barracks, ships and schools

5. the religious retreats from the world of monasteries and con-
   vents.

For several generations people who were slow learners have
been directed into the second kind of total institution, usually
when the families could not provide for their needs. The
obvious task of these institutions was to feed, house and clothe
their residents, and to protect them from harm and exploitation. There were other motives: one was to hide away from

society those of its members who seemed unable to conform easily and so puzzled and frightened society by their behaviour and appearance; and another was to ensure that people with mental handicaps were denied any sexual life. For many years there was a wholly incorrect belief that they were liable to produce large numbers of retarded children, and there was a public horror of the possible effects on society. This idea, popular in the 1920s and '30s, encouraged the building of many British and American institutions in the country, where men and women were segregated. In America compulsory sterilisation of some women with learning difficulties continued until quite recently in some states. The provision of institutions for people with intellectual and other disabilities was society's method of catering in the cheapest way possible for their bodily needs, of protecting society's eyes from what it did not want to recognise as part of itself, and ensuring that the imagined population explosion of slow learners was prevented.

Whether the total institution is a barracks, a mental hospital or a prison there are major characteristics of the life lived there, common to them all, and which influence all the people within, both inmates and staff. It has already been noted that normally life is lived in separate sections such as home, work and leisure. In a 'total institution' all those parts to life occur in one place and are controlled by one authority. They are not independent or private from the other parts. Each phase of daily activity is always carried out in the company of a number of other people who are all treated alike and are expected to do the same things together. The schedule of changes from one activity (or inactivity) to another is arranged by other people and imposed from above. The various enforced activities are designed primarily to fulfil the official aims of that institution, not to meet individual needs. For example, activities are often timed to fit the convenience of the catering department in a hospital. The fundamental characteristic of total institutions is the handling of many human needs by the bureaucratic organisation that groups the people in blocks. Those people are all expected to fit in to the pattern of conduct of the whole block. There is a firm division between the large controlled group of people labelled inmates (or residents), and the smaller group of people labelled supervisory staff. Inmates live all the dimensions of their lives publicly in the institution, while staff are present for institution shifts, but then return to their own domestic settings. The relationship between inmate and staff is made very clear by the use of either first name or just surname for the inmate, but Mr X or Sir for staff.

In Chapter 7 the importance of work in people's lives was described. A total institution provides everything for its inmates, housing, food and clothing; and although work may be demanded of the inmates, that work does not have the same purpose as in the world outside. The work is not done by an inmate on his own behalf but at the behest of the institution. The motivation and the rewards therefore are different. Thus a member of the armed forces receives pay but not specifically for the work he does; he is paid to work, sleep and even play around each 24 hours. Some of the make-work activities deliberately introduced can show time and effort to be worthless. A mental handicap hospital has the responsibility to provide for *all* the physical needs for its residents; the value of their work is thus only to keep them 'occupied' or, occasionally, to train for some undefined future. Any payment is 'reward' money or pocket money.

When an individual joins a strict institution he undergoes certain common experiences. In prisons today, for example, a number of things are done to the prisoners, and the same experiences were undergone in the past by long-stay patients in old mental handicap and psychiatric asylums. National Service recruits to the army and religious novices recognised the same processes also. The individual is systematically dealt with by the institution so as to destroy the sense of 'self' or individuality. The process includes the breaking of previous relationships and breaking with the past. By a variety of means the individual is stripped of personal possessions and made to appear the same as everybody else by wearing identical clothing (uniform) and haircuts. There is no privacy of actions or thoughts as sleep, hygiene, dressing and toilet are all conducted in the company of others and under staff control. Every activity or lack of it is under the surveillance and judgement of staff; there is no choice about anything. Decisions are made by others. Inmates are required to be respectful and subservient to staff.

Once in such a strict institution they will find that simple things in life they normally had taken for granted become 'privileges' which must be earned from staff by rules which can be very arbitrary. They will be punished by the loss of privileges or the opportunity to earn them. Inmates of strict institutions cope with this demeaning process in a variety of ways: by withdrawing into themselves and becoming inwardly inaccessible; by becoming permanently unco-operative, 'bucking the system'; and by joining the staff, that is to become a 'trusty'. Forming close relationships with other inmates can be supportive but the institution usually sees these as too threatening and will break them up.

The reasons why people have arrived in such institutions and the time they spend there varies widely: for those in prison or in the army there is a fixed period after which they return to the outside world. In Britain 45,000 people who are slow learners were placed in institutions years ago and for them an outside future disappeared. Their admission to the institution was quite as destructive of individuality, initiative and close relationships as prisons. Although mental handicap hospitals are greatly improved from 20 years or more ago, there are still some where lavatory doors are not closed, women wear pants also worn by others and men are shaved with communal razors. Nevertheless, the deliberate process of mortification has stopped.

All the time it must be remembered that these residents are

by definition very slow learners and the lessons they so agonis-
ingly learnt about life long ago will never be unlearnt easily.
Men and women in their forties and fifties have spent 20 or 30
years in a system which punished any demonstration of individuality (unless it amused the staff, for example as a 'clown'),
and removed any need for responsibility for self or others, and
any sense of real purpose in life. It removed any opportunity to
experiment or to learn from ordinary living. Most profound,
perhaps, was the lack of experience of close reciprocal relationships; of *being* as well as *having* a lasting friend; the capacity to
empathise, that is to feel *with* as well as *for* another. In the institution people are always around, but there is no means of being
alone with a friend. Thus caring staff will sadly comment on
very many residents that they are 'loners', and they will sometimes attempt unsuccessfully to create relationships artificially.
Such individuals lacked the bonding opportunities until it was
too late in life, or else over the years learned it was safer or easier
to live without close relationships.

Even among people of normal intellect it is recognised that
several years in a strict institution produces a state of 'untraining' which leaves them temporarily or even permanently incapable of managing some aspects of daily life outside. This
condition results first from being removed from the everyday
lessons in living outside, and second by the practice of activities
in the institutions which are inappropriate in the outside world.
Residents in long-stay hospitals demonstrate their state of
untraining in all sorts of ways. Both obvious and subtle, they
cover areas of practical knowledge, but also in social skills and
in emotional development. Such damaged individuals are
termed 'institutionalised'.

So far this chapter has described what institutional life can do
to the inmates. Institutions contain staff, too, from colonels
down to corporals, whether they either be actually soldiers,
gaolers, nurses or nuns. In their various ranks they are expected
to keep the institution running on behalf of their masters who
may be the Ministry of Defence, the health authority or a board

of governors. No such institution is designed or intended to put individuals first, but to meet needs collectively, and staff are expected to keep the institution running smoothly. This is achieved best by standardising things, meal-times, clothing, activities, timetables. Staff attempting to change routines face enormous obstacles from the total system, their bosses, colleagues and other departments, for example, 'The evening meal must be at five o'clock as the catering staff go off after that.'

Changed routines even if for the benefit of clients or residents are very disruptive and therefore to be resisted. The institution also is expected to be *efficient*, that is to get more out of the money spent on it. Being efficient is not the same thing necessarily as being *effective*. Caring staff have constantly found themselves in conflict between providing for the personal needs of their clients or patients and having to find ways that are quicker or cheaper. Shared garments were not only a way of diminishing individual identity but a quick cheap way of clothing and laundering *en masse*. Even now although the residents in most mental handicap hospitals have their own clothes they are made of fabrics to suit hospital laundering.

The hierarchies of staff in such organisations form a pyramid with status and respect expected from the layers below. The fewer the layers or ranks left in the pyramid from which to extract personal respect the greater is the insistence with which it is demanded. One of the most important ways by which people learn is by the process known as modelling, that is copying consciously or unconsciously how others do things. In staff hierarchies people are aware that officers, or sergeants or staff nurses or students act in certain ways, and if promotion is hoped for that style of behaviour must be adopted, as it is apparently what the institutional system values. The behaviour and standards which are displayed at the top of the organisational pyramid set the model for what happens at the bottom of it, and that goes below the level of the lowest staff member to the actual inmates themselves. Where staff feel disregarded from above and without control of their own working lives, that model will be inevitable for their relationship with those below them – the residents.

Research has shown that in systems where staff feel over-controlled and under-appreciated those caring staff are unable to retain a warmth for their job or their clients over any length of time.

Most of the big mental handicap hospitals were deliberately built in the country and housing for the staff was part of the estate. Staff recruited to the hospitals formed small villages and today they may consist of close interrelated social and family networks covering three generations of staff, as relatives, friends and enemies. So although hospital residents have to remain on the wards all their lives, large numbers of hospital staff also may live all their lives in the social world of the institution with its customs and attitudes. The more isolated such a community is, the greater is the resistance to inevitable change. Such resistance to change also maintains a considerable sense of security and this is threatened with the movement to community care.

A large hospital is a source of employment or income for many people and may be the only local industry. Recognising the ill effects of institutional life on *residents'* development has led services to think hard about how to enable such people to live like anybody else in ordinary houses, sharing or watching household tasks, leisure pursuits and work. In planning such moves for clients, for whom after all the service exists, the needs of staff and their problems in coping with change must be recognised and catered for.

Not only is new knowledge needed, but fresh ways of reaching targets have to be tried. For example, staff working in hospitals have been trained to work with and for *groups* of residents. Sustained, intensive individual work with the residents is not the model they have been trained in and the need to remain in one-to-one interactions with the same client over a period of time can be unexpectedly taxing.

LEAVING THE INSTITUTION

For a number of years now, adults have been moving in small numbers out of institutions into smaller accommodation. They have all been able-bodied and the most competent of the hospital population, capable of attending to their own bodily needs and of avoiding common dangers. They almost all have problems with money, number, reading and writing, but so do many of the ordinary population. These individuals usually win through the half-way house stage to a place of their own. They spend one or more years in a hostel or a training home before moving again to share an ordinary dwelling with three or four people in a group home, somewhere in the community. Occasionally the moves have been ill thought out and individuals were unable to cope with the arrangements. But leaving the institution and being able to make decisions about their lives has for almost all clients been an experience they would not reverse.

With hindsight it is possible to identify two features of that process that now appear curious mistakes to have made. The first was the way in which three to five adults were collected and placed in a house to live together with little or no systematic testing in advance of compatibilities, or of temperament and tastes. Ordinary family units evolve from people choosing one another to live with. Friends select one another and even then may not wish close proximity under one roof. Somehow the group home members selected (usually by professionals) were not seen to be as individually choosy as other people. Hence some homes demonstrated internal tensions which could be seen as inevitable where personalities were incompatible, but also, sometimes, were due more to the lack of awareness and practice of the give-and-take skills of adult domestic life. Residents in institutions have had much space in which to avoid emotional contact with others, and may have comparable problems experienced by staff when sustained contact is required. Individuals and groups can be helped by counselling, dis-

cussions and practice sessions (role play) to relate more com-
fortably to one another.

The second mistake was to train people in several settings;
people with major difficulties have them increased when their
lessons are taught in a mixture of places. The traditional pattern
would be learning to cook in the occupational therapy unit and
then in the pre-discharge villa, then maybe in a hostel and
finally in their group home: that is four possible kitchens with
four different training schemes. Time, effort and confusion are
saved if the individual can do his serious training in the setting
he will settle in.

However, these are two examples of the ways in which the
planning of services can continue to develop and improve if we
are prepared to go on learning from our successes and mistakes.
Nevertheless, the concept of considering people's individual
needs as the focus around which services are moulded (instead
of deciding whether people fit into what is available) is *very* difficult for traditional organisations like health and local authorities. There is still an overwhelming temptation to plan ways
of enabling institutionalised people to move out of hospitals
into accommodation which happens to be already available.
What is offered may be physically vastly superior to their previous hospital, but neglect of other human requirements leads
to problems and a sense of failure in the client, staff and system.

The third group of people after the clients and the staff, who
are involved when institutional residents move out into the ordinary world, is of course the general population. About 4
people in 1000 of the ordinary population of all ages have a
severe intellectual disability. Three out of that 4 always live in
the community anyway. It is the 1 of that 4 who is usually to be
found in a hospital, having arrived there years ago for a variety
of reasons.

The concept of providing the support and care that some
people need, in their own local communities, not in some segregated environment, means that those individuals must be enabled and supported to return to the ordinary world. They are

likely to have a mixture of severe disabilities, but all of them can be helped, given the appropriate skilled supports. In the face of local anxieties about hospital residents moving out to be supported in ordinary homes, it is important to remember that we are talking about bringing back only one person into every thousand of the population.

Despite the examples often quoted of disastrous hospital discharges into American city streets, there are excellent examples of how to cater well for people with severe disabilities in all local community settings which have operated in parts of the USA for 10 to 15 years. The Americans have a term 'de-institutionalisation'. It means, partly, the system of getting people out of institutions, but even more it is the development of an alternative, comprehensive network of support in the community so that nobody needs to go into an institution to live. As a figure of speech, they explain there is little point in trying to empty the bath (the institution) through the drain (discharges) if the bath is continually refilling through the taps (admissions)!

A comprehensive service which meets needs for a place to live, occupation, leisure, emotional and social supports, can only be based on individual assessments of such needs (see Chapter 4) and a commitment to supply the ingredients, individually and locally.

REFERENCE

Goffman, E. (1961). *Asylums*, p. 16. Now published (1970) by Penguin Books, Harmondsworth.

FURTHER READING

Raynes, N. V., Pratt, M. W. and Roses, S. (1979). *Organisational Structure and the Care of the Mentally Retarded*. Croom Helm, London.

Chapter 11

Sexuality and Personal Relationships

As more people with intellectual disabilities live their lives, or start their lives again, within society, they will include people who may have extreme perceptual difficulties. The subtleties and sophistication of present society in terms of technology and human relationships, are often a problem for average members of society, let alone those who are slow in learning. People seem prepared to cope admirably with the disabled so long as their image is not threatened, but any disabled person who threatens the comfortable view that society has of them is likely to find extreme difficulties, as are the carers. The image that society seems most able to cope with is one that is both patronising and asexual.

In previous chapters we have tried to show that the fundamental humanitarian values we attribute to ourselves must be allowed for the mentally handicapped.

This chapter will not give many answers, but it will raise some fundamental questions. It would be totally wrong not to discuss what we feel is the reality of the situation today. Almost every intellectually disabled person is being cared for by someone, a parent, brother, sister or friend, and many earnestly hope that their charge will not show too much interest in sex and sexuality. They should not feel they are alone in this for the professional carer is no better.

We have seen from other chapters the problems that mentally handicapped people have about social interactions – they are not alone. All of us from childhood are experimenting with social relationships. Our skill develops through exposure either directly or indirectly, and often by mistake! We can gain experience and insight through media such as TV, reading, cinema, and so on; if we do not understand we try and discuss what things mean so we absorb them into our lives.

COMMON FORMS OF SEXUAL BEHAVIOUR

In order to make sense of the issues involved in this chapter, let us begin by trying to identify what is usual in terms of sexual/personal behaviour.

There are many personal and moral standpoints relating to sexual matters: some people see sexual relationships as solely heterosexual, others see them as solely homosexual, others consider either or both acceptable. There is no 'normal' sexual behaviour pattern, though there is evidence to suggest heterosexuality is the most common factor. This is the standard 'family model' and some people see sexuality in that context as being for the purpose of reproduction coupled with fidelity; others do not. Some see and use sex as purely for fun – the list is endless. So why should society wish to see mentally handicapped people as asexual?

What are the dilemmas?

The basis for this particular attitude tends to be found in the history of mentally handicapped people. Unfortunately it has not received much publicity. It is possible that the antagonism shown or supposedly shown by people towards the intellectually disabled may well be heightened if awareness of their sexual activity was increased. To try and find an answer to this dilemma we must look again at the segregation of disabled people. They were removed from society either in their own interests or the interests of society and the latter causes concern. One reason can be found in the attitude of the eugenics movement; the anxiety that mentally handicapped people would produce a weakness within society and would reproduce to such an extent, because of their supposed excessive sexual appetite, that the world would be full of disabled people. This so-called fact was reinforced by the practice of segregating the sexes in institutions.

As a result of such living, was it really surprising that many institutionalised men and women displayed homosexual activity and showed a very limited ability about social function? While this segregation fortunately rarely exists today, these attitudes within society still do.

Eternal child model

Another factor is the view that mentally handicapped people are 'eternal children' and that children must be protected from exposure to sexual practice.

The need to expand society's views about mentally handicapped people is vitally important, but if one continues along this road of the 'eternal child' syndrome then it can be seen almost as a rational argument to suppress the sexuality of mentally handicapped people because they do not know any better. A responsible active sexual life requires an insight into responsibility and an expectation of social competence which can be learned. There is also the question of consent and the law, both of which will be discussed later in the chapter (p. 133).

It is only a short step away from saying that because we think they are not competent we have a responsibility to stop them becoming the victims of their own behaviour.

SEXUALITY

Sexuality is not limited just to sexual practice. Sexuality is more often an expression of tenderness and empathy with another person – a want and a need to share an intimacy with another soul. A relationship that may be deep and all-embracing. It is being aware of one's sexuality. It is about romance, tenderness, closeness, love, compassion and friendship: the experiences that possess all our minds, the need to care and the need to be cared for by others, the closeness of a deep personal relationship, the warmth, comfort and security that comes from this closeness. For all of us it develops through a social process and experiences that are a part of everyday life and a part of our lives that we feel is ours by right. We would not accept a practice that forbade us that right, and it is perhaps the consequence of exercising that right that causes concern.

It is amazing to report that even today there are people who have spent 30, 40 or 50 years of their lives in an institution for no other reason than becoming pregnant and having an illegitimate child. This situation was a result of legislation at the time – the Lunacy Act of 1890 and the Mental Deficiency Act of 1913 being the major factors. Within the classifications of mental defectives were two parts which were relevant. Many single women finding themselves pregnant were in danger of being classed according to the Act as either 'feeble-minded persons or moral defectives'. This judgement was probably based on their slow learning capacity and possible behaviour at the time. A major aspect of the Mental Deficiency Act was the increased number of persons certified and detained in hospital. The children of such relationships were often put into the care of the local authority and later adopted.

If we relate that to today's society, we should have to start building a new series of institutions that would require millions of pounds and many years to establish.

Lack of knowledge

Although the authors know of women who, because of illegitimate pregnancy, have spent most of their lives in institutions, they do not know of any of the fathers of their children being so punished.

There are others, particularly youngish men, who have a desire for sexual relationships and whose behaviour is limited. Through lack of understanding and help, they sometimes make inappropriate sexual advances to women and their actions are often seen as attempted rape. Their knowledge of sex is so limited that they probably couldn't achieve intercourse if the partner was willing. The young men often appear in court – pleading guilty and not knowing why.

Sexual conduct

There are many people who manage today's services who find themselves in what can only be described as a 'Catch 22' situation. Take the go-ahead unit, hospital or institution, that recognises that people are sexual beings, and suppose that this establishment introduces a formal sex education programme. Many would say it was correct and proper, others would condemn it. The managers are only too well aware of the effects on them, their service, its reputation and integrity, if the organisation is given bad publicity about this activity. Unfortunately few services will admit publicly to sexual education programmes for their residents and those who do can expect to go through the mill. Those who say they don't – are they truly fulfilling their function? Those who say they don't and do may get caught and what shall we expect to be done?

It takes courage and integrity to develop an appropriate, positive sexual education programme. While many of the organisations in this country have adequate training staff their curricula for sexual education and training are virtually non-existent. Why should this be?

Surely it is an expectation on the part of society that the intellectually disabled, like the rest of us, abide by the appropriate rules governing public sexual conduct and this, like so many other things, has to be learned. The development of a sexual education programme must be seen as positive. It should be appropriate, meaningful, lawful and dignified.

So where is the problem? It is important that all involved in the field of mental handicap attempt to promote the positive aspects and consequently we should try to dissect the reasons why sexuality and mental handicap seem incompatible. Perhaps we should try to give a less anxious and far more realistic view about intellectual disablement and the fact that handicapped people are also sexual beings. If there is prejudice about this problem it is mainly because of ignorance. Perhaps we should ask ourselves, is there a real problem?

Intellectually disabled people generally do not have sexual problems because most people who influence their lives tend to support an asexual attitude. What would society tolerate? People would probably accept that the intellectually disabled should behave within the law. If one looks at the number of sexual offences committed by intellectually disabled people, compared with other members of our society, then one sees that they are indeed in a very small minority. However, one sexual offence by any such individual and all are seen as the same.

What are seen as normal systems?

What would allow an intellectually disabled person to grow up and live within the normal system, be it at home or elsewhere, that would not only assist him to be aware of his own sexuality but also to appreciate what is and what is not appropriate and sociably acceptable? We have to remember that slow learners do not have the same facilities for development and education as ourselves. The information that might assist them tends to be removed from their range of learning opportunities. It is important that in any education programme one attempts to make sure that it is approached at a level of understanding for each individual. The eternal child model is fine, but intellectually disabled people are not eternal children. We all have a responsibility to make sure that appropriate behaviour is taught and understood, as lack of it will lead to social rejection. In many cases appropriate modelling and counselling will resolve many conflicts.

There are many problems facing the disabled individual, including the subtleties of interpersonal relationships. How often do these fail us? How many times have we failed truly to grasp the significance of a comment? How many times have we seen, or have had odd relationships within the normal spectrum and what is that normal spectrum? It is also worth asking ourselves how we may look to those disabled individuals and how they may view us. What are the norms for us – do we take our cues from TV and films? The more one looks at this complex subject, the more one can see the reasons for encouraging asexuality and perhaps one way to start is to look at our own learning system.

Until the last few years the majority of young people in Britain were not able to have access to formal sex education through the state system and so the majority of sexual learning was left to peer groups, observing society around us, by dirty jokes that amuse children, even when they don't understand them, and by secret conversations. Some children are more fortunate in having parents who attempt to capture opportunities arising in day to day living to explore, comment on or modify behaviour. The average child mixes in society and is thus able to pick up cues and to see sexuality all around.

These children live in a world of men and women whereas this hasn't always been the case for the intellectually disabled. As we have said before, there are still mentally handicapped people who have spent large parts of their lives in institutions where the sexes were segregated; for them the peer group offers no insight. TV or films may offer them the wrong information or their understanding of them may differ from the normal. Their learning opportunities are extremely limited and any expression of sexuality is suppressed. That applies not only to people in care, but also to those at home. The intellectually disabled person is not attributed with sexuality: it raises too many questions.

We set out on our own sexual development, armed with truths and half-truths, attempting to make some sense from this mass of information. Physically we start to mature: we change, our bodies change, it is difficult to make sense of our bodies. The physical maturity we reach is just the same for the intellectually disabled. We should remember what it did to us, how we coped, what we did, what happened when we got caught. For many people their sexual awakening is associated with discomfort and embarrassment.

The intellectually impaired do not suffer as we do; their sexual activity and behaviour are not tied up with the connotations and interpretations that we suffer. They do not always have the benefit of our counsel or the counsel we received as children. It is doubtful if anyone has ever explained matters to them. All they know is that when certain things happen they get a certain response. Take, for example, a multiply handicapped male tied up in his nappies because of his incontinence. Imagine the pain and discomfort of an erection: he may be labelled a behavioural problem.

As stated earlier, one area of concern is the lack of inhibition among the mentally handicapped, and a common problem is their masturbating in public or some other inappropriate place. The mentally handicapped person may find such activity greatly pleasing – always immediate and desirable, the consequences pretty obvious. Appropriate training and opportunity play a very important part in the resolution of such behaviour, but a starting point must be the acceptance that, given appropriate conditions, such behaviour is acceptable.

Imagine, for instance, a young man or woman who has discovered enjoyment in masturbation. It is not so much what is being done but where. It is obviously not acceptable in public places or at school or work. If this behaviour is shown more at home then asking them to go to their bedroom might be an immediate solution. Saying no in other situations may then be all that is necessary. At work or school other factors may help, such as provision of positive and active tasks that keep them well occupied. If that fails somewhere private may be a short-term solution. Exclusion from work or school is no resolution as more time then becomes available. A well-constructed and agreed programme of management is required if the situation is to be sensitively and positively resolved.

Contraception

Effective contraception is now a part of everyday life. Contraceptive advice and information should form part of an overall counselling programme where all the benefits and disadvantages are taken into consideration and discussed fully with the people concerned. Individual help is best provided by an organisation such as the Family Planning Association whose considerable experience and sensitivity will be advantageous. It is important that contraception is not seen as a means of relieving the anxiety of others, but related to the needs of the mentally handicapped person. Many methods are available and common sense should prevail. In our experience, barrier methods such as condoms have not proved very successful. Teaching their use has proved difficult, particularly for physically disabled couples. Until recently, intra-uterine devices were commonly used but this method is now declining. Since the advent of oral and injectable low-dose hormonal contraception this has shown a high success rate and to be an acceptable alternative.

Marriage

Marriage is another area of difficulty. Many mentally handicapped people in recent years have shown a desire and have, in fact, become married. If the legal requirements are met then there is no impediment to marriage. Many of these couples have experienced great difficulty in obtaining suitable advice about their joint emotional development and the development of their sexual relationship.

Parenthood

Linked with this is the question of parenthood. The decision about contraception versus sterilisation versus parenthood is one that can and should be taken only by the couple concerned. Historically many mentally handicapped women of child-bearing age have been given oral contraception without their knowledge and some have been sterilised without being fully consulted.

In our experience, there are some mildly mentally handi-capped women who do desire children and given support would cope, but without support could well face major difficulties. Sometimes in these circumstances the child is taken into care, prompting the desire to replace it with another. This is obvi-ously a tragic situation. Appropriate help, advice and support systems might be more helpful than resorting to the removal of a greatly desired child. Some resolution to these problems must surely be found. Intellectually disabled people will, in future, be living alongside us in society and we must, for our own good, and particularly for theirs, be more constructive. At present there is some very positive action being taken in attempting to work through these issues in various parts of Britain.

WHAT NEEDS TO BE DONE?

The London Borough of Hounslow in 1981 and Derbyshire County Council in 1985 both produced guidelines for staff involved in services for mentally handicapped people. A report was drawn up for the Social Services Committee, mainly to draw members' attention to the controversial areas surrounding the topic. The guidelines on the sexuality of mentally handi-capped people in Hounslow were eventually agreed in Novem-ber 1982. The main force behind this development was that staff recognised the need for a policy not only for themselves, but for the residents. There was an involvement with parents and an attempt to ensure support from them. The parents did express a great deal of anxiety. A most frequently expressed view was that it would potentially implant sexual awareness when none had really existed.

This is understandable because of the possible consequences that such a training programme might bring about. An extensive staff training and counselling service was established. Their guidelines covered the following areas – parental involvement, sexual intercourse, petting and masturbation, plus the legal position with regard to the Sexual Offences Act and intellectually disabled people.

While not wishing to provoke situations that may lead to gross exploitation, one cannot accept the present state of things. If one looks at the education of intellectually disabled people one can see that further urgent development is required. For those presently undergoing de-institutionalisation there is a cause for extreme concern with regard to their personal development. Many man-hours are invested in the assessment and training of these people about the development of normal behaviour. We teach them how to make cups of tea, we teach them how to dress themselves, we teach them how to do many things, we encourage development in every area *except* sexuality. It is sexual behaviour or potential sexual behaviour that society finds so terribly threatening.

THE LAW

Introduction

The legal situation is extremely complex and the authors here merely give the background and some direct reference to statutes. At the end of this chapter there are some suggested publications, advisory services and services that may assist. These notes relate to England and Wales only and are not intended to be comprehensive but to give the reader some basic insight. This information we believe to be correct at the time of going to press (1987).

Right to make decisions

Every citizen from the age of 18 years (including mentally handicapped people) has the right to make his/her own decisions.

Acts of Parliament

There are five Acts relevant to sexual matters and mentally handicapped people:

Sexual Offences Act, 1956
Sexual Offences Act, 1967
Sexual Offences Act, 1985
Mental Health Act, 1959
Mental Health Act, 1983
plus the Mental Health Amendment Act, 1982.

Age of consent within society

From the age of 16, heterosexual intercourse is legitimate. Men may enter homosexual relationships at the age of 21. At 16 people may marry with parental consent, change their doctor and decide on their own medical treatment. At 18 an individual can marry without parental consent.

Sexual Offences Act, 1956

It is unlawful under the Sexual Offences Act for a man to have *unlawful* sexual intercourse with a woman who is a defective (Section 7) or for anyone to procure a woman defective for unlawful sexual intercourse with any man or men (Section 9).

Marriage

There is no law specifically restricting marriage with regard to mentally handicapped people over the age of 16 with parental consent, or without consent over the age of 18, so long as the officiant is satisfied that both parties agree.

Divorce

Divorce is the same for all.

Consent

In general terms, mentally handicapped people are as capable as the rest of us at making choices and, with assistance, of giving consent. Mentally handicapped people need to be helped to understand the consequences of their actions. How this is done, and the extent to which the consequences are elaborated, where these are in any doubt, must be matters of joint decision and agreement.

Two specific legal aspects that relate to people with a mental handicap are:

(a) neither a severely handicapped man or woman can give consent which, for any other person, would prevent any act from becoming an indecent assault (Section 14(4) and Section 15(3), Sexual Offences Act (1956));

(b) Section 1(5) of the Sexual Offences Act (1967) states that a man suffering from severe mental handicap, within the meaning of the Act, cannot in law give 'consent' to homosexual acts.

Section 1(2) provides that an act which would otherwise be treated for the purposes of this Act as being done in private shall not be so treated if more than two persons take part or are present. If a mentally handicapped person is under 16 then parental consent is required for all things, but from the age of 16 they are able in law and in principle to give their own agreements.

FURTHER READING

Craft, A. and Craft, M. (1982). *Sex and the Mentally Handicapped: A Guide for Parents and Carers*. Routledge and Kegan Paul, London.

Craft, A. and Craft, M. (1983). *Sex Education and Counselling for Mentally Handicapped People*. Costello (Publishers) Ltd, Tunbridge Wells.

de la Cruz, F. and LaVeck, D. (eds.) (1973). *Human Sexuality and the Mentally Retarded*. Brunner-Mazel Inc, New York.

Greengross, W. (1976). *Entitled to Love*. National Marriage Guidance Council, Rugby.

Greengross, W. (1980). *Sex and the Handicapped Child*. National Marriage Guidance Council, Rugby.

McCarthy, W. and Fegan, L. (1984). *Sex Education and the Intellectually Handicapped*. Williams and Wilkins, Baltimore.

Available from the Family Planning Association, 27–35 Mortimer Street, London W1N 7RJ: *Personal Relationships and Sex Education for Mentally Handicapped People*. Workshop Report, Rugby 1983.

Dixon, H. and Gunn, M. *Sex and the Law*.

TRAINING MATERIAL

Bodies

Available from Family Planning Association (Education Unit), 27–35 Mortimer Street, London W1N 7RJ:

Sexuality and the Mentally Handicapped. 9 slide presentations for teaching the mentally handicapped individual. Devised by Winifred Kempton MSW and Gail Hanson. Distributed by SFA, Santa Monica, California.

Chapter 12
Staffing Issues

A large majority of people with a mental handicap live either with their families or on their own, often requiring very little help or support from professional services. At different times in their lives they may need to call upon one of the services for support. The quality of service they obtain at such times depends on many factors. They must first of all gain access to the service which is appropriate to meet their needs. Provided they manage this then the particular professional assigned to deliver the service must bring with her a wide range of skills, attributes and attitudes which will ensure that the desired outcome is achieved through a high quality service. In practice the quality of service is largely dependent on the individual who delivers it.

For people with a mental handicap who have chosen to be supported away from their family, or who need to leave the family home for whatever reason, dependence on professionals for support is likely to be much more critical. Although this group forms a minority there are still thousands of people with a mental handicap in this position. Some require support throughout the day and night with almost everything being done for them. Delivering a good personal service to someone who is almost totally dependent is extremely demanding. In these cases professional support staff become the cornerstone on which a good life for the client is built. It is vital that planners and managers of services also take a close look at the needs of their staff and try to find ways to meet those needs.

STAFF SELECTION

It used to be said that people who entered the 'caring' professions must have a vocation. The implication was that such people were 'born' rather than 'made' and that entry into the caring role was very much a process of self-selection. Pay was usually poor or non-existent and new skills were learned from the experience of actually doing the job. As the delivery of care and support became increasingly a matter for the public services (see Chapter 2) this led to the professionalisation of the workforce.

The first step in providing a high quality service (workforce) is the initial selection of staff who seem likely to develop into people who will have the right skills and attitudes. There is no foolproof method of assessing people to ensure they have the right attitudes. Even if their written applications and all their responses at interview increase one's confidence that they will turn out to be good staff, one will only really be in a position to assess them once they are working with their particular clients.

Most people will have seen how important are the relationships that develop between client and staff in determining what the quality of service will be for any individual. Although it is possible to obtain some general impressions through the selection process about how individuals are likely to relate to others, it is important to help them monitor their performance and feelings in their everyday work and to help them realise that they are not failures because they find some clients difficult to relate to. They may need to explore more carefully *why* they are having problems. They may need an opportunity to work in another area with other people to whom they can relate more easily. Whatever the solution for the individual it is unlikely that these difficulties could have been predicted by the selection process.

Managers and planners, perhaps with years of practical experience to draw on, often set up jobs which they believe will achieve a desired outcome. Even if they are correct in their assumptions and decisions and the job specification does enable many of the needs of individual clients to be met, it is most unlikely that they will find a selection process that will lead to the appointment of staff who consistently match that specification. Each person is unique and in supporting others one is likely to have to deal with thousands of situations which were not predicted when the job was set up. Staff need to feel they can respond flexibly and, if necessary, negotiate to change the job to take account of their own needs as well as those of the client. Changing a job routine to accommodate an individual is likely to be far more successful than attempting to change the personality and behaviour of each staff member. Where certain basic standards can be identified it is obviously important to set clear limits and to help staff achieve them through training. On the other hand it is likely to cause havoc and lead to a poor quality service if a job cannot be changed to suit individual staff.

STAFF TRAINING

Each professional employed to deliver a service to people with a mental handicap must have training which is based upon the most up-to-date knowledge in the field. As a starting point, regardless of their chosen profession or the level at which they are likely to operate, they should be helped to have a clear understanding of the underlying philosophy on which the service is based. There is an increasing awareness that people with a mental handicap are at the centre of services and that it is only from this starting point that a service can be designed (Chapter 4). Each person must be viewed as an individual with rights and responsibilities similar to those that any of us expect to have as ordinary citizens. The service should then be designed to give the level of support required to permit the person to exercise those rights and responsibilities, as far as is possible, without placing them at unnecessary risk.

The training which follows from an understanding of this basic philosophy should be designed to do two things. Firstly, it should provide skills and knowledge which are directly relevant to the job that is to be performed. In the past too much time has been spent in training for some recognised qualification where the course content has included much that is irrelevant to future job performance. Second, the training should build upon the agreed philosophy so that it is brought to life. The philosophy must be transformed from theory into practice. It is pointless having a well-thought-out belief about the way people with a mental handicap should be respected as individuals if the practices encouraged through training prevent individual care being given.

All staff working in a particular area should undertake a common core of training which is clearly relevant to the area in which they work. There is now a much clearer understanding of what things might make up such a common core. The provision of services to people with a mental handicap has been influenced over many years by a variety of important factors (Chapter 2). This historical perspective should be used as an introduction to current thinking which has begun to emphasise the importance of the values held by society and those who work in services. A common set of values which accepts the person with a mental handicap as a respected individual with the rights and responsibilities of an ordinary citizen must be developed and shared as a basis for all staff training.

Assessment leading to the delivery of an individually tailored service within the available resources is central to any high quality system and all staff should be helped to understand the basic elements of such a process. The needs of any individual cover a wide range and must be accurately identified before decisions can be made about service supply. The majority of staff in a service, regardless of their particular day-to-day jobs, need an understanding of how such needs can be identified (Chapter 4). This does not require them to become experts in the use of complicated assessment techniques. Such special assessments may be required occasionally for particular purposes but these would be carried out by the specialist in that area. What is required is for all staff to get to know the individual (or individuals) they work with most and to be sensitive to what that individual tells them about his/her needs. It is often difficult to learn to 'hear' what an individual tells one, particularly when that person has a very limited ability to communicate in the usual way. It is even more difficult to 'hear' if there is already a strong preconception of what his/her needs are, particularly where this is based on one's own beliefs. All staff must learn to avoid prejudgement and to recognise their own biases.

The underlying philosophy and the assessment process will identify many needs for individuals who may require considerable support in many areas. Direct care staff will have to have a range of basic skills including home management, simple first aid, handling of difficult behaviour, helping with social integration, and so on. These skills must be supplemented by an ability to teach as many of them as possible to the person with a mental handicap. All of this may sound like the sort of thing that all reasonably competent parents learn to do with their own children. In practice, however, most parents rarely achieve the level of skill and patience required to support a mentally handicapped adult for many hours of her life while enhancing her personal dignity and worth, which highlights the necessity for this common core of training.

INSTITUTIONALISATION

There is considerable evidence (Chapter 10) to show the effects on people who become institutionalised by the system in which they operate. The main thrust of the evidence has been to demonstrate the effects on those who have to live in institutions. It is equally true that staff working under the demands placed on them by the institution come to behave in ways which are now described as institutionalised.

Institutional practices which gradually minimise the opportunities to treat people as individuals carry the inherent possibility that standards of care will fall and can in turn lead to unintentional abuse. Staff require help and support to combat institutional pressures so that individuals with a mental handicap can remain at the centre and genuinely influence the care they receive. Many of the steps which can be taken to reduce the effects of institutionalisation upon staff are quite simple.

Staff at all levels must be encouraged to minimise the distance between each level as well as that between them and those whom they support and care for. The absence of official or unofficial uniforms, the way people talk to each other as respected human beings, and a close link with ordinary communities all help to avoid the worst forms of institutionalisation. Where possible routines that require individual treatment must be supported and such routines should be similar to those of any ordinary person. Staff should be encouraged to form genuine relationships with clients rather than using excuses such as 'staff turnover' to justify maintaining 'professional distance'. In general any steps which lead to staff being valued and given true control over as many of the aspects of their daily routines as possible will minimise the effects of the institution.

BURN-OUT

A modern phenomenon identified as applying to staff working in the caring professions has been described as 'burn-out'. This is viewed, for example, by Cherniss (1980) as the response of individual staff members to stress and strain experienced through the job. In the first stage of burn-out, the demands of the job are greater than the person's ability to meet those demands. It may be that the person does not have the skills or ability to carry out certain tasks, or there may be insufficient time or a lack of personal energy which prevent completion of the job. In response to this situation the person is likely to become anxious and to suffer tension, fatigue and exhaustion. This is seen as the second stage, which leads on to actual changes in the way the person treats the clients, as well as alterations in attitude towards both the job and the clients.

This three stage process, called burn-out, causes the individual staff member to withdraw from personal interactions with clients and to treat them in a detached, often uncaring way. Staff become preoccupied with protecting their own welfare by 'going by the book', avoiding change or progressive thinking and generally losing interest in their work. There is likely to be an increase in minor illnesses and time off work. Relationships with other staff, including other professionals and line managers, are likely to deteriorate so that suspicion and even paranoia replace trust and co-operation.

In the field of mental handicap in the last few years the pressure has grown to view people with a mental handicap as developing individuals who can learn new skills which will enhance their chances of becoming independent. This has been a positive and important step in changing staff attitudes but it has placed the emphasis heavily on the staff. Whereas in the past the lack of progress in an individual was attributable to his/her mental handicap it is now more logical to argue that it is the absence of appropriate teaching. By implication this throws any failure back on to the staff. It is no longer acceptable simply to provide good care. The goal to be achieved is the observable improvement in the level of specific targets, ranging from simple self-help skills to the most complex social behaviours. By these outcomes success is measured.

Conversely, success is also measured by the absence of difficult and disruptive behaviour. The recognition that at least a proportion of difficult behaviour is determined by the individual's response to the environment and the environment's response to that individual has again placed the staff at the centre of the search for causes. Much of the advice given to direct care staff to help them manage difficult behaviour also demands a change in their own behaviour. Implicitly staff must feel criticised either for doing the 'wrong' things, which triggered or maintained problem behaviours in their clients, or for failing to do the 'right' things, which would have avoided the development of the difficult behaviours in the first place.

If one accepts that all staff need to achieve personal success in their jobs and to feel that their efforts are rewarded by the outcomes in their work, then it is not difficult to understand why the above view of people with a mental handicap could lead to their feeling they had failed to achieve any personal accomplishments. From this viewpoint the measure of success for the job is based on the progress of the individual with a mental handicap. The greater the level of impairment present in the individual the more difficult it is to achieve this type of success. The teaching skills required become more complex and the change in an individual can be so slow, even with the best teaching methods, that the measurement of positive change is almost impossible.

To overcome this it is important for managers and planners to find ways of defining each job, in genuine consultation with the direct care workers, in a way which ensures that staff can succeed. The job should be made up of a series of tasks that are well understood by the person doing the job. Ideally each task should be defined sufficiently clearly so that anyone assigned to it will know how to carry it out and when they have completed it successfully.

In some services efforts have been made to provide a detailed written analysis for every task. These show the exact steps which make up the task and offer a precise guide to the procedures that should be followed. This approach can give valuable help to staff. It is necessary, however, to ensure that the natural, essential differences between people and the way they respond to each other are not swamped. A balance is needed which could be described as a process of 'flexible consistency'.

The consistency ensures the best opportunity for individual clients to feel secure and for learning to occur. The flexibility ensures a place for individual differences, both in the staff and their clients.

Management must also find a way to help people feel they are a success. It is very easy to treat staff in a way which devalues them. Peters and Waterman (1982) note that organisations often 'call for risk taking but punish even tiny failures'; they punish verbally any signs of poor performance; they 'want innovation but kill the spirit of the champion'; they 'design systems that seem calculated to tear down their workers' self-image'. What is required is a system that reinforces each successful step rather than simply emphasising failures. Failures must be dealt with in a constructive way rather than by handing out punishments and abuse.

In every organisation there will be some people, usually a small proportion, who are more interested in securing their own ends and who will cheat the system in some way to achieve this. If managers assume this is the norm, they will design systems to catch out the cheats. The message received by all employees from such systems is 'we do not trust you'. If there is any danger of burn-out such a message will help ensure that it occurs. Yet the large majority of people are trustworthy and keen to succeed positively. People need a work context which gives them an opportunity to be best and to receive their just rewards. In short, to be valued human beings in an organisation that provides a high quality service.

Organisations that provide a service must recognise and acknowledge that the staff are their most important asset. The senior managers must provide clear guidance on the limits within which workers are expected to operate. Those limits should come from a relatively small number of values which can be shared explicitly as basic truths. The truth of these values must be demonstrated and reinforced through the whole range of interactions that occur between managers and staff. Managers should not only be approachable and accessible but

should spend time with junior staff in their workplace providing them with information, listening to them and attempting to understand their views and suggestions. At the same time
this provides an opportunity to give positive feedback and reinforcement for even small successes.

Seeking out and rewarding the successes takes practice. In
organisations that provide a personal service the essential small
successes can become lost and treated as unimportant. Worse
still they may even remain unnoticed. The completed house-
work, the routine provision of good food, the help needed to
ensure excellent standards of personal hygiene and dress all
become 'invisible'. It is only a *failure* in these standards which
makes its mark on the observer. The routine achievements
need reinforcement if they are to remain as routine. Staff themselves must also be helped to recognise and acknowledge their
own achievements. Any mechanism that helps with this should
be encouraged.

It is not always the demands made by the organisation that
set the scene for burn-out to occur. Staff almost always set their
own goals within their job, particularly when they first start. In
their early enthusiasm they may set goals which are unrealistic
and standards that are so high that failure is almost guaranteed.
This can also happen when staff receive training away from the
realities of the workplace. Training which involves staff in challenging their old attitudes and practices and then returns them
to the workplace without providing practical solutions to help
them achieve their new expectations can once again guarantee
failure. Although apparently self-imposed, this gap between
the demands of the job and the resources needed to achieve the
desired outcome, can provide the conditions for burn-out to
occur.

Staff need to be helped to set realistic goals for themselves.
They must first recognise the limits set by the organisation, the
available resources and their own skills. Awareness of these
limits can help them make realistic decisions about goals to be
achieved. The process described as 'Individual Planning'

(Chapter 4) requires staff to agree to carry out tasks to help achieve clearly-defined goals to meet the needs of the person with a mental handicap. If this exercise is conducted in an open and realistic manner by everyone involved and participants regularly ask each other if they can really expect to achieve what they agree to, it can help everyone to work within sensible limits. This is not to say that there are not times when identified limits have to be challenged in the interests of improving the service. The important decisions here are which limits to challenge, how to make the challenge and when the challenge is most likely to succeed.

The very nature of the relationships that have to exist in caring situations can lead to frustrations which result in feelings of anger and eventually violence. The person with a mental handicap is likely to be placed in a position which, because of his dependence on others, is inferior and the person providing the care and support is likely to place a range of demands and expectations on him. The potential for conflict is high. Conflict is also likely to occur between staff and their co-workers or line managers. Most staff do not have an opportunity to learn skills to help them resolve these conflicts. When conflicts do occur it is difficult to learn directly from them. Feelings are usually running high, with anger and frustration preventing positive learning from occurring. There is usually no opportunity after the event to review what happened in a dispassionate way. Most people would need considerable help to carry out such a review even if they had the time. More work needs to be done to help prepare them to avoid conflict wherever possible and to have strategies to deal with it should it arise.

Examples of typical conflicts which could occur should be used during training to help sensitise staff to the factors which might signal potential conflict in their work. Staff must learn techniques which permit them to remain calm and relaxed even in the face of unrealistic demands and pressures from others. For example, many conflicts arise because as one individual gets close to being aggressive or violent another provides signals which can act as a trigger. With practice it is possible to learn to control anxiety and anger and to give bodily signals which are calm and calming. It is important, for example, to avoid unexpected or rapid movements and to maintain a posture which does not carry any threat. Talking in a quiet but clear voice about things usually helps to reduce tension.

A typical conflict can arise where a staff member giving direct care and support decides on a course of action which threatens the policies or philosophies, written or unwritten, of senior managers. If an individual with a mental handicap has spent many years in a particular form of residential care, she may have learned to sit for long periods on a child's swing. The concept of age-appropriate behaviour which is encouraged by senior managers may be clearly contravened when the person in charge of the residence encourages a local charity to pay for the broken swing to be replaced. A careful appraisal of this type of situation makes it obvious that neither of the opponents is offering an ideal solution. To prevent the person's having access to a swing after so many years, particularly where there is no direct cost to the service, could have a devastating effect on her and on the whole routine of the residence. To replace the swing as an automatic response to the old one's breaking could be to miss a golden opportunity to help the person reappraise the way she spends her life. The solution to such a problem which will avoid a conflict may require considerable effort on the part of both sides to work calmly together and with the individual to help her reduce her dependence on the swing while increasing her ability to take part in alternative, more appropriate activities.

The examples of conflicts used in training can be coupled with a number of possible solutions for staff to discuss. Most conflicts are complicated and experienced staff are likely to have several different solutions which could produce a resolution. New staff should have the opportunity to discuss these situations and solutions and if possible to practise their own responses through role play.

The new ethos in organisations is towards efficiency,

effectiveness and accountability. The concept of staff appraisal is once again rearing its head. This can be viewed as a management tool to keep an eye on workers to make sure they are as efficient as possible. Alternatively a process of regular appraisal can be used to provide workers with positive feedback on their performances and to help them explore any sources of frustration or pressures which could lead to burn-out. Provided there is a positive, trusting atmosphere developed by both sides towards staff appraisal it should be possible together to identify the problems and to take steps to change the job to reduce stress and increase work satisfaction. Where an individual is helped to identify the problems there should be an opportunity, if required, to receive further counselling. Such counselling should seek to help the person break out of the spiral of depressions and seek out the positives in their job. Changes in the attitude of the staff member may be essential before he can be of help in bringing about changes in his own job. Often the very act of helping a person become conscious of his/her difficulties can provide the important first step towards positive change.

The jobs one expects people to do are usually the end-product of a complicated process of evolution. The organisational requirements, the needs of the staff and the needs of the client interact to produce staff performances which often settle down to become the lowest common denominator. Over time the emphasis or pressure from one set of demands may increase or decrease with a corresponding shift in the work output, but in general an equilibrium is likely to be achieved which can adjust to these changes. This may encourage everyone to stand back and avoid disturbing the balance while trusting to luck that the service that results is acceptable. In practice, however, it is likely that, unless there is a determined effort to keep the welfare of both the client and the staff at the centre of developments, the pressures of the organisation or system will determine what a job looks like.

A practice that has become popular is to assign the role of key-worker to an individual staff member. This usually entails one person's having clear responsibility for a small number of clients. With this responsibility goes the freedom to develop a close relationship with the individuals and to make decisions about the way many of the day-to-day routines are achieved. All of these features of the key-worker role can contribute to a reduction in staff burn-out as well as providing a more personal service to clients.

Cherniss (1980) states that 'research has suggested that differences in the quality of supervision and leadership account for more of the variance in burn-out than any other single factor'. This seems to agree with the converse statement that high quality performance goes hand in hand with high quality leadership. One feature of good leadership which is likely to have a major impact on staff morale and burn-out is the ability of a supervisor to make staff feel they are valued. This can be achieved through a range of techniques, including positive feedback for success, seeking and listening to the views of individual staff, giving staff as much autonomy as possible so that they can experience some level of control over their jobs, or simply being regularly available to staff in the workplace. It is all too easy in a field of work which places the responsibility for the lives of vulnerable people in the hands of staff who have often had a minimum of training, to have supervisors who meet their own responsibilities by hiding behind strict policies backed up by punitive, controlling, autocratic methods of ensuring the policies are followed. This may help the supervisor feel in control and safe from public criticism but it will do nothing to contribute to a better service and will dramatically increase the chances of staff burn-out.

SUMMARY

Carefully selected staff need regular and relevant training within an ethos which provides clear values and helps the individual to set achievable goals. Supervision must be through positive monitoring with informal, face-to-face communication. Staff must *be* valued and *feel* valued. Senior managers must understand and take steps to overcome the problems of institutionalisation and burn-out. Staff are the most valuable resource in human services. Every effort must be made to sustain and develop this resource if high quality services are to be guaranteed.

REFERENCES

Cherniss, C. (1980). *Staff Burn-out: Job Stress in the Human Services*. Sage Publications Inc, USA.

Peters, T. J. and Waterman, R. H. (1982). *In Search of Excellence: Lessons from America's Best Run Companies*. Harper and Row, USA.

Chapter 13

Causes and Prevention of Secondary Disabilities and Handicaps

One of the principal themes of this book is that all people, whatever their genetic make-up, disabilities or experiences, continue throughout life to be responsive to changes, and that we all remain capable of personal growth throughout life. For people with disabilities, life is an unending process of change and adjustment as it is for anyone else. The state of 'being alive' consists of interactions continuously occurring between the unfolding genetic programmes inherited in the chemistry of each cell, with ever altering environments of all kinds. In all body cells genetic instructions are programmed to 'switch on' and 'switch off' biochemical activities at times which vary over the day, the month or the years. The various processes of childhood growth, of sexual maturity and of ageing are three major ones which are 'switched on' and 'off' during a lifetime. The likelihood of the genetic programme's being fulfilled depends on the environment being healthy, and enabling the process. The nature of our genes, of disadvantages and experiences, influences the nature of global development. Richly enabling environments can sometimes nurture surprising levels of personal growth in the face of major disabilities.

From conception to death, the capacity to survive or succumb in various adverse environments can rise and fall: this is partly dependent on genetic make-up, partly on past history which gives acquired characteristics to the individual, and especially on the degree of environmental hostility. Any adverse event will vary in its impact, depending on the stage of life at which it occurs. Comparable brain injuries, or biochemical disorders, will not necessarily affect adults as they do children. The earliest phases of life are the most globally vulnerable to hostile influences, and much effort is now made to ensure a safe, well-nourished, infection-free environment for children before and after birth. This is part of the programme of *primary prevention* of disabilities.

During the first few years of childhood exceedingly complex interactions evolve between a rapidly enlarging body with its maturing nervous system and muscular strength, and the immediate environment over which the child is gaining some awareness and control. Each new behaviour acquired by the young child in one area of development is the foundation for further progress in another: bodily maturation, external opportunities and increasing skills all contribute to rounded development. In this way there is integrated progress in sight, co-ordinated movement, hearing, communication, social and emotional development and the ability to make some sense of the world experienced by the child. Serious damage or deprivation in early life can impair and therefore distort the child's physical development, leaving the child hampered in his learning in cumulative ways. The recognition that difficulties accumulate sequentially is most important, if they are to be avoided or ameliorated.

Failure in the past to recognise that despite the severest disabilities people continue to grow and change, has led to layers of secondary and tertiary handicaps being added over a lifetime to their initial problems. These secondary and tertiary handicaps arise from acts of omission and of commission in their support over the years. Some of the omissions were inevitable, due to lack of technical knowledge. Certain biochemical impairments are now chemically treatable and brain damage avoided if the conditions are identified sufficiently early in infancy: children with deficient thyroid function will, if untreated, become cretins, and those with the genetic disorder phenylketonuria

(PKU) are biochemically unable to digest protein, which leads to brain damage when untreated, but identification at birth followed by special regimes will protect normal development in each case.

Impairments and disabilities are not static and if unaided will usually produce further complications. A baby with cerebral palsy is initially very floppy, and only later develops muscle spasm; then that uneven muscle tension over years may lead to uneven skeletal growth, bones fragile from disuse, damaged joints and restricted respiratory movement, all of which render the individual more vulnerable to ill-health, and disadvantages. People who have Down's syndrome are particularly vulnerable to infections, and as a result catarrhal deafness is common. When this is unnoticed the individual can become chronically isolated from sounds, so compounding his learning difficulties. Such secondary complications must always be borne in mind, and action taken to avoid further disabilities.

Deprivation – acts of omission – have contributed to secondary and tertiary handicaps. The lives of many people, now middle aged, who have Down's syndrome can provide ready examples. When they were infants their parents received little help for the child's special needs and were usually advised not to expect any development beyond that of a child of 7. Parents proceeded to raise their sons and daughters with little support, in an expectation of 'perpetual childhood'. The children became adolescents and then adults, but under conditions of intellectual and social deprivation since they were denied exposure to opportunities and experiences only available to people older than 7.

Many such men by 27 had not learned to bath or shave themselves, make hot drinks or cross the road alone, simply because those skills do not apply in a child of 7. Adults have grown up incompetent and dependent, knowing they are perceived that way by others; not because they are innately incapable, but because they have been prevented from learning. While many adults welcome the opportunity to acquire the skills later, some are found to have learned to enjoy the dependent role very thoroughly, and others can find the anxiety of change very painful. When people have grown up incompetent in basic self-care and social skills due to failure of teaching and opportunities *we* have created secondary disabilities, and in destroying expectations of an *adult* role, *we* have given them secondary handicaps.

Tertiary disabilities and handicaps are the results of deprivation and damage inflicted by segregated and institutionalised lives; examples are described in Chapter 10. Sometimes residents in such settings have not only experienced deprivation but acquired physical disabilities from restrictions on movement.

During the last decade a start has been made on raising public consciousness of the need to *en*able those who are *dis*abled. Some improvements have been achieved in attaining access to ordinary public facilities for people with physical disabilities, whether they result from cerebral palsy, road accident, multiple sclerosis, or stroke. The help available can range from hip replacement surgery to electronic equipment or public toilet access. For several years now there has been a welcome improvement in attention to the mobility and wheelchair needs of physically and intellectually disabled children: their problems are obvious and merit concern and understanding.

There is however another disability, much more common among people who have severe learning difficulties, which still remains virtually ignored. The enormity of its significance stays invisible because it is silent: many people with severe intellectual disability cannot speak.

Humans are the most social and highly communicative animals on earth. Spoken language has evolved only in humans and has enabled mankind to control his environment and himself, to share his ideas and his information with others, about the past and future as well as the present. We put enormous value on talk, and live in a world of words. Communication is an ability held by many species, including birds and bees; what is communicated by animals and insects, however, is available only from a fixed range of messages; there is no creativity. Parrots and mynah birds can speak, that is imitate human voice sounds, but without any meaning. *Language* is a far more complex activity than either communication or speech. It is a system of *symbols* – sounds, gestures, pictures or written words with a capacity for infinite combinations and expansion. Language provides limitless communication possibilities across time and space, of private individual ideas and feelings and of whole cultural traditions. Learning to think involves the manipulation of symbols (words, sounds, pictures, writing) which represent past experiences, and in that thinking process we can learn what we did not know before: we can predict and plan for the future.

The use of language has three essential parts.

1. *The sender*, who must 'encode' what he needs to convey into gestures or expressions, sounds, drawings, writing, smoke signals or drum beats.

2. The *communication channel* so the message can cross from sender to receiver. These will include sound waves, light and Braille patterns, as well as print, telephones and transport.

3. *The receiver*, who must be able to receive the signals, and then 'decode', or make sense of them.

Successful communication therefore requires several things. The sender must be able to 'encode' the message and then express it in a form understood by the receiver. A child can have learned to *understand* spoken, gestural and even written language from others, but if cerebral palsy affects the speech or hand muscles he is unable to express himself in reply: his thoughts and feelings are locked in. The receiver must first be able physically to receive the encoded message, to hear, see or feel it, and then to be able to 'decode' it, from the knowledge of what the words, sounds, gestures or print represent.

Deafness and blindness block two routes of communication and together create a silent darkness. It is considered by some that total deafness is a worse disability than blindness; that being unable to hear and talk with other people creates far greater isolation than not being able to see them. Apart from possible associated problems in physically sending or receiving communications due to sensory or speech impairments, people who are severely intellectually disabled have varying degrees of difficulty in encoding, decoding and using information. For a few there is a profound difficulty in learning to relate to other people at all. Although there may be difficulty in decoding (that is understanding) the words of others, however, the associated *emotions* conveyed by voice pitch or gestures are likely to be received more readily, and may produce perplexity and anxiety, if the meaning of the words is lost.

Human beings use language to control their environment (including their social environment) and themselves. When the psychological relationship between any individual and his environment breaks down, social and emotional disorders are likely to develop. In the ordinary population the capacity of individuals to understand and influence their bit of the world varies to a large extent with personality, education and experience; so similarly does the ability to cope with failure, disappointment and anxiety. Some will accept disappointment as a challenge, others will be diminished by it. Some people who in growing up have been actively discouraged from talking about their inner feelings and how they view their world will, if faced with chronic frustrations and conflicts, 'act out' their anger and despair by injuring themselves, others or property. People who have an intellectual disability have been described as normal people who have more learning difficulties than most of us: 'normal' people develop anxiety states, become aggressive or withdrawn or difficult when their capacity to cope with life's problems is diminished. In view of the secondary and tertiary disabilities and deprivations experienced throughout the lifetime of most slow learners, the long-suffering and patience they display is awesome, but it is hardly surprising that some people with severe difficulties, including communications, by the way they behave and by their emotional state suggest a condition of chronic hopeless frustration. Mabel Lucy Attwell, the pre-war cartoonist, once drew a small lonely boy crying to the moon, 'I don't know what it is I wants, but I wants it awful bad.' Disturbed emotions and relationships are harder to resolve if words are not available to identify them. Chapter 4, 'Assessment', shows how from early in life we learn to describe the world around and within us; that we are taught ways to tell others and ourselves what we experience and how to label those experiences. What happens to people who do not understand words or cannot speak them?

People who are intellectually disabled are as liable as anyone else to develop psychiatric illnesses and severe emotional disorders. In some individuals, varieties of brain pathology or seizure disturbance will contribute to their disordered moods and activities. In a person with severe learning difficulties who is never enabled to become competent or respected, however, the sense of incompetence, frustration, bewilderment, hopelessness and humiliation must inevitably lead to degrees of emotional disturbance and distress; that is a very important variety of secondary and tertiary disability, seen especially in mental handicap hospitals.

It is commonly this secondary emotional disability, with its failed relationships and despair, which has sent people into mental handicap hospitals and made them patients of psychiatrists: as a result 'mental handicap' continues to be confirmed as a sub-specialty of psychiatry, and remains unadopted by the more appropriate profession, that is, education. Chapter 10, on 'Life in the Institution', suggests why corporate hospital life is unlikely to provide the individualised opportunities needed by such a disturbed person for full habilitation. Some psychiatrists and other colleagues, find they can now apply both their treatment and their preventive skills more effectively in small ordinary settings, away from long stay hospitals.

A range of disabilities which interfere with global development has been identified in this chapter; it includes disorders of locomotion, hearing, vision, intellect, communications and emotions. The harmful effects of all of them can be tackled by the application of modern skills in teaching, treatments and technology. Attention has also been drawn to the *handicaps* (disadvantages), added to the learning difficulties people already have, by depriving them of ordinary opportunities to learn. These disadvantages include the failure to recognise the universal potential for growth, the assumption of low expectations, and the practice of segregation.

It is accepted that the presence of primary impairments and disabilities will inevitably influence growth and development through life: what is to be done to minimise all the possible secondary and tertiary disabilities and handicaps? What are the goals to be aimed for? It has been suggested elsewhere that all children should be able to reach adulthood with a sense of personal identity, a good self-image, and a sense of belonging; able to discriminate, make choices and exercise direction over their lives and remain alert, curious, imaginative, stable and flexible enough to tackle and solve problems (Heron and Myers, 1983).

The goals of education for very slow learning children have been debated since it became their statutory right in Britain in 1970. Until recently their only expectation on leaving school has been an ATC place, being a 'trainee' until 60. There have been no expectations of leaving home, paid employment or marriage, so no efforts have been made to achieve them. But, the first generation of children with severe learning difficulties is now receiving statutory educational provision and their parents are claiming support for them.

It is urgent that we stress the capacity for continuing learning and personal growth into ordinary adult roles. We all learn our adult roles in ordinary human environments, from one another, and those *ordinary* environments (not segregated ones) are where the adults with disabilities *must* function, with personal support as indicated. Ordinary adult social and work behaviours must be promoted: the passive acceptance of child-like behaviour from a disabled adult, gives an additional handicap (disadvantage) by diminishing ordinary adult status. Discrete and courteous suggestions of alternative greetings or activities together with an example to copy, may be all that is required to enable an individual with severe learning difficulties to be received and perceived as nothing other than 'ordinary'.

From early childhood onwards, while brothers and sisters prepare for adult work and relationship roles, the disabled child is excluded from any plans for his or her own future home, occupation, marriage or self-determination. The issues do not arise, except as a source of sadness and regret. The status of permanent childhood or asexual semi-adulthood is assumed without much question from early in life. Paediatricians, teachers, trainers and social workers share the parents' assumptions that young people with severe learning difficulties cannot learn to make choices or share in serious human relationships.

There are many adult roles which as individuals we judge to be inappropriate for ourselves and we choose to avoid them. People with intellectual disabilities need the opportunities to consider the possible options, their implications and to make their own choices, too. The role of spouse or close companion should be an option available. Parenthood is understandably the one role parents immediately discard for their disabled sons and daughters, but it is impressive how adults with severe learning difficulties can recognise for themselves the tremendous demands child-rearing makes, and express a positive choice not to have children.

People who are intellectually *dis*abled need to be *en*abled to function in mutual interdependence with other people in the ordinary domestic, work and social settings of their local community, thus experiencing a sense of self-worth, belonging and growth. All efforts to avoid secondary disabilities and handicaps at the individual and at the organisational level must be directed to these ends.

REFERENCE

Heron, A. and Myers, M. (1984). *Intellectual Impairment – the Battle Against Handicap*. Academic Press, London and New York.

FURTHER READING

Ellis, D. (ed.) (1986). *Sensory Impairments in Mentally Handicapped People*. Croom Helm, London.

Chapter 14

Difficult and Inappropriate Behaviour

This chapter attempts to identify and discuss what might be termed difficult and disruptive behaviour which may cause distress and alarm resulting in destruction of property or injury to self or others.

Disturbing interactions of this nature are not solely the province of the person who is intellectually disabled. Although many people associate this type of behaviour with a stereotyped mental handicap, one has only to read a newspaper or listen to a TV news programme to see so-called 'normal' members of our society engaging in a variety of unacceptable behaviours. The normal development of many people shows periods of difficult or disruptive behaviour, with most children from a few weeks of age into adulthood exhibiting patterns that may cause anxiety to parents and in some cases society at large.

Many young children learn behaviour patterns that succeed in delivering things they want. Children in supermarkets screaming for sweets are a good example, or children sitting down in the street throwing a tantrum. Society tolerates such childhood behaviour and dismisses it as normal within this age range. Society's view would be different, however, if the 4-year-old child, behaving in such a way, was replaced with a 15-year-old. The major problem for the parent, apart from acute embarrassment, is that if necessary one can carry a 4-year-old away. Ageing parents trying to do that to a 35-year-old man would have little chance of success.

An obvious social aspect of such behaviour is that it tends to reinforce the negative social view of people with mental handicap. One common solution for parents is not to get into the situation in the first place by not going out among others. The price for such action is social isolation.

The following example may help demonstrate what would be considered difficult and inappropriate behaviour:

> A 14-year-old boy is a constant menace – running up to men and women in the street and throwing his arms around them and kissing them. It is such a problem that his parents are concerned that someone will beat him or cry rape, maybe not today but eventually. From early childhood he has been encouraged to engage positively and emotionally with people. His parents and grandparents used to encourage him to climb on their knees, put his arms around their necks and kiss them. He and they enjoyed the interactions. It was only when he was getting bigger they found it was becoming a problem, mainly because he would behave like that with everyone he met. When he was a toddler people responded positively, as an 8-year-old he was embarrassing. At 14, because his behaviour is not appropriate for his age, he frightens people and they feel threatened. He finds it difficult to understand why, because for many years it was welcome. He feels unhappy, rejected and confused.

NORMAL LEARNING OF BEHAVIOUR

Human behaviour is extremely complex. Mature behaviour is learned through a series of interactions, which teach one how to react to a variety of situations. Many books have been written on this subject. Perhaps the one that stays in many people's minds is Desmond Morris's *The Human Zoo*.

Over many years the sophistication of basically crude experiment and knowledge about the modification of behaviour has been developed. People have attempted to identify the reasons for patterns of behaviour which cause people difficulty, such as bereavement depression or certain learned behaviour.

All individuals grow and develop from continuing exposure to everyday life. Some of the messages received are quite blunt and brutal and responses are likely to be crude and simple, but in our complex society interactions, messages and stimuli are frequently far more subtle and complex. Even for people of normal intellect the ability to sort out what is being said is difficult – we may hear the words but the message may be quite different.

In attempting to describe the lives of people with mental handicap the phrase 'a stranger in his own country' has been used to describe some of the difficulties. People reading this book have so far received hundreds of thousands of stimuli so that they can understand what is written. The road to enlightenment, knowledge, behaviour, maturity has had to be learned. Though extremely complex, lessons about social interaction, have modified our behaviour. It has been modified by parents, brothers and sisters, teachers, as well as newspapers and television. All these images, all these messages, have been absorbed in order that we can make sense of society and our particular position within it.

There have been times when everyone has struggled, so it is no wonder that the intellectually disabled person has even more problems in trying to understand and make sense of this complex web.

As previously mentioned the reasons why people (not just those with a mental handicap) might demonstrate difficult and disruptive behaviour can be many. What we do know is that environment, people and experiences play the major role in our behaviour patterns. It is the modification and manipulation of these factors that have resulted in an approach called *behaviour modification*. It is often very successful, and throughout this chapter reference to terms used and the principles underlying this technique will be explored. (A glossary of some of these terms is on pages 175–7.)

One common historical approach was to label people with a mental handicap as disturbed, disruptive or aggressive and consider such action part of their condition. It is now widely recognised that such people feel and respond to the same emotions as ourselves.

In attempting to identify the reason why a person behaves in a certain way it is important to start with some basic information. To gain insight into the unacceptable behaviour one needs to ask when, how and what is the effect, when does the unacceptable behaviour occur, and what form does it take. Some examples of disturbed behaviour could be self-injurious behaviour, aggression, constant running away, non-co-operation, disruptive behaviour shouting or screaming. This part of the assessment process is known as *Base Line Information*. By recording/charting the behaviour one may identify certain patterns that emerge. Objective versus subjective information is required. Because communication is often a problem for mentally handicapped people careful assessment is vital, if only to exclude possible physical or mental illness. Areas to consider are:

PHYSIOLOGICAL/PSYCHOLOGICAL CAUSES – PAIN

One of the most common causes of difficult and disruptive behaviour is often overlooked – that of pain. If you can imagine yourself with earache or toothache that had lasted for 24 hours without treatment you would probably concede that your behaviour towards family and friends would be somewhat altered. Mentally handicapped people, like ourselves, become ill but their ability to explain how they feel is often difficult for them.

There are many chronically painful conditions and some acute that cause distress to all of us.

CONDITIONS RELATED TO MENTAL HANDICAP SYNDROME

There are some conditions that, apart from causing mental handicap, also produce changes in the individual body. They are not always present, but do occur commonly with different degrees of severity. Examples can include phenylketonuria which is often seen in over-activity of the individual. Another condition, that of Lesch-Nhyan often presents the feature of self-mutilation.

Other physical conditions, such as brain tumour, abnormally functioning thyroid, some types of epilepsy, can all cause an altered state of consciousness and an alteration in behaviour.

MENTAL ILLNESS

Anxiety/depression is not uncommon. It is often triggered by changes in lifestyle or the death of a loved one. This grief is often ignored as too sophisticated an emotion for mentally handicapped people to experience. It is nevertheless a very common disorder and responds well to conventional therapy. The amount of severe mental illness associated with the mental handicap is difficult to assess fully and more research continues to be undertaken, although its prevalence is noted as a reality. The major difficulty is in the diagnosis of such conditions because discussion with the individual is a key element in diagnosis. Although a fair amount of research of severe mental illness associated wth mental handicap is being undertaken, there is still need for further research.

DRUGS

The use of drugs in mental handicap has in recent years been undergoing review. The use of drugs in controlling behaviour as opposed to other techniques is a debatable point in need of much more research. The risk of side-effects versus achievement in controlling behaviour requires careful thought. Parents and professionals are particularly concerned about the use of major tranquillisers and their use is less acceptable and more of a last resort than a first option. The use of barbiturates for the control of epilepsy and for sleeping is rare, as the side-effects often outweigh the advantages.

DIET

Though little research is available to date, modification of the diet of those who are mentally handicapped has produced remarkable results in some sensitive individuals. Particularly interesting is recent research concerning hyperactive children. This research by the Department of Immunology and Child Psychiatry at Great Ormond Street Hospital, London, on hyperactive children showed that colourants and preservatives were the commonest substances that provoked abnormal behaviours (Flack, 1985). While additives may not be a primary cause they may be the trigger mechanism required to produce unusual behaviours. Some foods promote other physical conditions such as migraine. Research continues into allergies.

ENVIRONMENT

This is a major area for analysis. In our own lives our environment is a major factor influencing our well-being. If we are unhappy at home, work or school the effects can be devastating.

Even when we are not in that environment our feelings associated with it remains with us, clouding our thoughts and actions. The environment in which people live is, of course, important but the actual building design can be over-emphasised at the expense of what could be seen to be more important factors that go towards the person's total environment. Within institutions these include people, privacy, availability of personal space, small numbers of living companions and access to a wider range of activities. The main characteristics which may be considered important in deciding on the environmental aspects of care for those with severe problems are:

1. the need for containment
2. the need for control
3. the need for consistency.

It is considered that these crucial factors should be taken into account before any attempt is made to change behaviour or introduce a training programme. They have important implications for where the training is given.

It is apparent that those mentally handicapped individuals who exhibit difficult and disruptive behaviours can be divided roughly into two groups: those whose behaviour presents a problem of such severity that they need, for a period, to be treated apart from the rest of the community; and others, the majority, whose behaviour presents problems, but they are manageable.

The aim, therefore, should be towards preventive practices so that the need for special facilities for temporary containment is reduced to the absolute minimum. Much effort needs to be put into dealing with the less severe problems so that they do not escalate into major ones.

BEHAVIOUR MODIFICATION/BEHAVIOURAL TRAINING

Behaviour modification is a teaching procedure. The aim is the positive one of producing improvement rather than the passive one of observing and explaining.

It attempts to teach individuals specific skills – skills which will help them to function more effectively, enjoy wider experiences, and to put them in a position to continue learning other valuable skills. The success of behaviour modification rests upon careful attention to, and arrangement of, the consequences of behaviour, as behaviour occurs mainly because of the effects it produces.

Learning (or any other change in behaviour) is most easily produced by careful arrangement of the consequences of behaviour. Recognition that the most immediate cause of behaviour is some characteristic of the situation, rather than some characteristic inside the individual, opens up the hope of behavioural change for people who exhibit unacceptable behaviours. The situation can be arranged so that it teaches constructive-meaningful behaviour instead.

The simplest statement of what is involved in using a behaviour modification procedure is that one should reward desirable behaviour and not reward undesirable behaviour. Behaviour which is rewarded, or reinforced, tends to be repeated, while behaviour which is not reinforced tends not to be repeated.

There are two types of goal which may be sought in the application of behaviour modification. The first is to teach the development of some new behaviour in the individual. The second is to eliminate some undesirable behaviour which the individual already displays. Identifying and teaching a positive meaningful behaviour which may be the direct opposite of the difficult or disruptive behaviour, lend themselves to a more constructive approach to reducing the occurrence of the bad behaviour. You are encouraging and teaching rather than stopping and punishing, which should be more beneficial to both yourself and the person with the mental handicap. For both teaching and eliminating behaviour, the methods depend on stressing appropriate consequences to behaviour.

CLASSICAL CONDITIONING

There is seldom a one-to-one relationship between a given stimulus and a given response. The same stimulus may well elicit different responses in different people, or it may elicit different responses in the same person under different conditions and at different times. There are some stimuli that always do produce the same responses. It was the regular occurrence of a given response to a given stimulus which first attracted the attention of the Russian psychologist, Ivan Pavlov.

Pavlov was conducting experiments relating to gland secretion, using dogs. The dogs, he discovered, were salivating when they were given food. Pavlov discovered that if the same circumstances and situation were created and the food was not present, the dogs still salivated. Pavlov, in these experiments, presented the dogs with bowls of food. He discovered that the dogs would salivate. He then moved to the next stage and rang a bell when the food was presented. Again the dogs salivated. In a short time he had merely to ring the bell and the dogs would salivate. What this experiment showed was that originally food equalled salivation, but within a short space of time, bell equalled salivation.

Classical conditioning involves a physical response. Another example is the development of phobias. For example, if a child is taken to a dentist and the experiences are unpleasant, then it is not too surprising to find that the child will very quickly become conditioned to being concerned and anxious whenever he is being taken to the dentist. The response may go farther and may just become a general anxiety of going into places with people in white coats, reminding the child of that distress and discomfort, which at that time was not only an emotional response but a physiological response to distress.

ORGANISATION OF THE ENVIRONMENT

There are features of organisation which are important for most people who exhibit difficult and disruptive behaviour. These could include a stable pattern to their daily lives, the presence of predictable and reliable human contacts, freedom from meaningless restrictions and fixed limits to behaviour with consistent consequences.

A regular and predictable sequence of meaningful events during the day increases the person's sense of security in which he/she can learn what limits exist and what he/she can expect to get out of his/her involvement in these events. The regularity of meal-times, work and leisure periods gives a structure to their day as it does ourselves. As with our own structured day, the structure should not be so rigid that it cannot be modified, but it should not be so malleable that it is not a structure at all.

People's feelings of security are always increased if other people's behaviour is predictable and consistent. We are well aware that we cannot expect to treat all mentally handicapped people in the same way, and we are likely to respond differently to different people at different times. These differences in reaction, however, should be within recognisable limits, so that the experiences with us will lead them to know what to expect. It is possible that the handicapped person may tend to be more vulnerable to, and less able to cope with, wide variations in our behaviour.

If there is a regular pattern to their lives, if they are able to rely on our reactions, and if they are able to predict what will happen from day to day, handicapped people are more able to understand their environment.

Many handicapped people have been bewildered by inconsistent events in their lives for which they have not actively been responsible, and which they do not understand. Unexpected changes become commonplace in institutions. These can result in raising the anxieties of clients, which are immediately apparent if they are asked to cope with unexpected events and unfamiliar situations. Where mentally handicapped people are in close and continuous contact with a restricted number of staff members, which is a feature of institutional life, the reliability of interactions is more in evidence for scrutiny and unreliability is, therefore, more noticeable.

This is an important feature of the treatment/training of people who exhibit difficult and disruptive behaviour. It is experience of predictable, consistent and reliable human contacts that so many of these people need, and it is the ground-work on which more particular or more specific forms of training can be based. For some people this ground-work alone is sufficient and can make a surprising difference to their attitudes and behaviour.

In our experience, this is borne out by people who observe changes in others, labelled difficult and disruptive, after a period of intensive treatment or environmental planning. It is not uncommon for observers to ask 'What do you do to these people?', when commenting on some improvement in behaviour. What we do is to provide experiences where more consistency, predictability and reliability are characteristic features of the client's environment.

There is another feature of reliability which is important for a disturbed person – the reliability of staff members who do not give way under the strains imposed on them. This reliability is needed in a staff's relationships with handicapped people generally, but it is particularly necessary in the relationship between a staff member and an individual handicapped person.

The organisation of the environment in which handicapped people live has to allow for freedom and flexibility so that staff members can respond appropriately to people's individual difficulties and needs, but fixed limits have to be set to prevent disorder and the possibility of damage to self, others or property.

Reconciliation of individual freedom with the need to put restrictions on freedom is a major problem for parents and staff in the management of difficult and disruptive people. The limits to be placed upon a person's behaviour need to be agreed among all persons concerned so that unanimity is assured. Inevitably people will test the limits and the ability of family or staff to enforce these limits. Difficulties can be caused if we agree to limits set, but then make exceptions. From experience we can say that limits are certain to be transgressed and the problem of what to do with transgressors raises many issues. It raises the question of whether punishment is appropriate or effective in controlling difficult and disruptive people.

One of the difficulties about punishment (by which is meant the deliberate infliction or provision of an unpleasant experience designed to produce acceptable behaviour to replace unacceptable behaviour) is that it seems to be more effective than it is. It does bring about changes in behaviour. It also reduces tension in the punishers who feel they have achieved something and altered matters for the better, but it is easy to overrate its deterrent effect. In a very real sense, punishment is most effective for those who do not need it.

Punishment of people who exhibit difficult and disruptive behaviour is a complicated matter, but there is a deceptive simplicity about punishment which is one of the reasons it should be approached with a good deal of caution.

There are, for instance, assumptions made about the effectiveness of punishment in reforming or deterring the behaviour of these people, and about their ability to comprehend it as retribution. Because punishment is likely to prevent or interfere in the establishment of the important relationships between the handicapped person and her carer and is likely to stir up hostility and resentment in people, those who base their role of care on the effectiveness of promoting good person-to-person relationships are not likely to rely on the use of punishment as a means of managing difficult and disruptive behaviour.

This approach is emphasised among those who base their work on psychodynamic concepts, but the advocates of social learning theory also argue that although punishment does change behaviour, it has many undesirable effects. It suppresses rather than eliminates behaviour.

TIMINGS OF INTERVENTION

It is sometimes better to delay an intervention when a person's misbehaviour is distracting so that the other members of the group can exert their influence upon the disruptive one.

Most clients signal the imminence of disruptive behaviour and the most effective intervention in these cases is to pick up the signals, so that the crisis does not develop. Observing the signals gives us the opportunity to defuse the situation. If the signals are unavoidable, it may be better to intervene and allow the crisis to develop at a time when he/she is most able to control events.

Interesting points about verbal interventions:

1. Humour, *if it is real*, and not a hostile comment disguised as humour, can be an effective verbal intervention in a tense situation; it demonstrates security and confidence if he or she is the object of hostile comment, and it provides an opportunity for both parties to relax. Sometimes, however, humorous interjection can misfire completely. A person could see it as mockery and find other peer group members' laughter unbearable.

2. Almost everyone dislikes being abused or shouted at or publicly reprimanded, and such interventions can stir up hostility and make disruptive behaviour worse. Sometimes a loud verbal intervention is unavoidable, but it is generally better to make quiet and effective comment where appropriate. A study of the effect of loud and soft reprimands on children's behaviour by O'Leary et al. (1970) showed that use of soft reprimands, i.e. those audible only to the child, reduced the frequency of disruptive behaviour and a few soft reprimands were more effective than many loud ones.

Timing physical intervention

If one has to move towards an individual who is disturbed it is usually better to do this quietly and unobtrusively. If physical contact is required it should be carefully managed so that it can in no way be regarded as an attack, and careful timing will prevent any hasty action which could be viewed as hostile.

Restraint or removal from a situation may be difficult to manage, especially if a carer knows he/she cannot manage it easily and successfully: much better not to attempt it. If a person is plainly out of control and nothing but physical restraint will prevent him from hurting himself or others, or damaging property and equipment, then he/she should remove other people from the area and seek assistance – remembering people come before property.

It is important for staff/carers to have some strategies prepared in case of emergency, should physical intervention be necessary. This increases their confidence, reduces the possibility of harm to all concerned and prevents excessive use of physical restraint where this is not needed.

Where people have to intervene and manage a physical intervention, it should be done in such a way that it does not communicate a physical challenge, which inevitably prompts counter-challenge. This is not always easy to do, and everyone should be aware that the line which marks off a specific and preventive physical intervention from an aggressive intervention is very easily crossed.

GLOSSARY

In any scientific type experimentation one has to understand the terminology used and so a short glossary of terms is offered.

Avoidance learning   The learning of any response that results in the avoidance of an aversive consequence, such as when a child will stop misbehaving whenever a person is present who has in the past used punishment to stop the misbehaviour.

Baseline   Measuring what a person can do before any intervention to change that behaviour – for example, we might record the number of evacuations on the toilet before a toilet training programme is started.

Behaviour   This refers to all the activity of an individual that can be observed by someone else.

Behaviour modification   This is the systematic use of principles and procedures derived from learning theory, particularly reinforcement theory in a teaching situation.

Generalisation   This refers to a process where behaviour that is performed in one situation is also performed in another. If we teach a child to name some objects in a special teaching room we should want this behaviour to generalise to the ward.

Intermittent reinforcement   A general term for schedules of reinforcement when the reinforcer is presented only intermittently. It can be on a number of different schedules such as fixed ratio or fixed interval. This programming of reinforcement produces behaviour that is more resistant to extinction than behaviour reinforced on a continuous schedule. A good example of an intermittent schedule is shown by the behaviour of people playing 'one-arm bandits'.

Negative reinforcement   The process by which a behaviour is strengthened when a negative reinforcer, or punishment, is removed. For instance, you might turn down the sound of a loud radio – the loud sound would be the negative reinforcer, turning down the sound would be reinforced by its removal.

Operant   A class of behaviours that can operate on the environment to some effect. It can generally be considered to be all that behaviour not included under the heading of reflex behaviour, although there are exceptions.

Operant conditioning   The process of training operant behaviour using reinforcement principles. Behaviour modification consists mainly of techniques derived from operant conditioning.

Positive reinforcement The process by which a behaviour is strengthened when it is followed by a positive reinforcer or reward. The process of giving the reward to make the chosen behaviour more likely to occur again is called positive reinforcement – for instance, we might pay attention to a child when he is behaving well in order to increase the number of times that occurs.

Prompting The help we give a child to show him what he is expected to do. We should use a lot of prompting initially to teach a new task and gradually fade it out so that the child can do it on his own. There are three main types of prompt – verbal, gestural and physical.

Punishment The process of applying a negative reinforcer or punisher when an undesirable behaviour occurs in order to reduce the frequency of that behaviour. There are so many dangers with using punishment that it cannot generally be recommended as a training procedure.

Responses The name given to a specified unit of behaviour – for instance, in feeding the filling of the spoon is a specific response in the whole chain of feeding behaviours.

Stimulus Any event in the environment of the individual to which he might or might not respond. A stimulus might be someone saying 'John, come here', to which John might respond by ignoring it.

Stimulus control When a given stimulus can be shown to control the occurrence of a specific response. Much of the training procedure involves building up new stimuli to control desirable behaviour. For instance, you want a plate of food to be the stimulus that controls eating behaviour, not other people's fingers or pieces of clothing.

REFERENCES

Flack, S. (1985). The hidden danger in your child's food. *You Magazine*, October 13, 24–8.

O'Leary, K. D., Kaufman, K. F., Kass, R. E. and Drabman, R. S. (1970). The effects of loud and soft reprimands on the behaviour of disruptive pupils. *Exceptional Children*, **37**, 145–55.

Chapter 15

When People with a
Mental Handicap Grow Old

The process of ageing has received a lot of scientific attention in the last few years and many depressing myths, assumptions about old age, have to be challenged as a result (16% of the population of the UK are retired people).

Growing, and being, old involves much more than bodily changes: it involves intellectual and emotional functioning, social relationships and how society regards its older members and why. The changes of ageing can be considered briefly under these headings:

PHYSIOLOGICAL (BODY) CHANGES

Bodily changes with age are not at all uniform. Some organs and tissues can remain in a much younger state than others, in the same person. For example, an elderly person may have fine smooth facial skin, but stiff joints; another may have hardening of the arteries although the stomach lining remains unchanged, and a third in her eighties may have a very lively mind although her hearing is impaired. Some of the changes have a genetic basis: a tendency to certain characteristics (such as longevity, smooth skin, etc.) runs in a family. However, health in earlier years is of enormous importance in avoiding chronic disability later. Healthier lifestyles in earlier years should lead to fitter older people in future years.

INTELLECTUAL CHANGES

One of the sad assumptions and myths about old age is that of 'losing one's mind'. The truth is that 95% of people over 65 are *not* demented. People over that age can show the ability to learn new skills and continue their intellectual functioning, and they vary in that capacity like any other people. Older people may *appear* to be less able than younger ones, because they have not practised certain activities for a long time, or because in their lifetime they never had the opportunity to perform certain functions taken for granted by younger people.

What is not widely recognised is that for a variety of reasons elderly people may become depressed, and that commonly looks like dementia. In addition, physical illness such as a chest infection, or mild heart failure, can make elderly people mentally clouded, and appropriate treaments for their physical conditions will restore their mental state also.

It is generally recognised that the best way to keep the brain functioning well is to keep on using it!

EMOTIONAL CHANGE

Any human lifetime may be viewed as a rope of intermingled 'careers' in various dimensions of living. Thus there is the work career (which is how the term is normally understood) with its promotions, changes, successes and failures, ending eventually in retirement. At the same time, though, there is the career as a marriage partner, that as parent, another supporting an aged father, still another as a grandparent, and in such personal interests as local politics, sport or other pursuits. These 'careers' have important effects on each other and may interrupt, diminish, or enhance developments in any area of life.

In later life the plait of such roles and relationships may remain thick and rich, but they can become thinned by geographical distances, deaths, separations, lack of purposeful occupations, physical disabilities and poverty. In a marriage one spouse may become physically and emotionally very dependent on the other, and possibly reverse the roles they have always had. It is hard that one partner may have to start providing physical care, when his own strengths are perhaps reducing. The death of a spouse may leave the partner without purpose in life, but occasionally the survivors may be seen to blossom unexpectedly in their last years.

A sense of purpose is an essential ingredient in our lives; we need purpose as we need food, and modern society starves older people of a purpose in life.

It has long been recognised that men whose self-image is wholly identified with their jobs can experience a terrible bereavement on retirement: similarly those women whose motherhood career was so dominant that other dimensions in life remained under-developed, can experience profound loss of purpose and uselessness when the last baby is no longer dependent. A prolonged sense of uselessness becomes severe depression and it is recognised that older widowed men figure high in the suicide charts.

Loneliness is a reality that can become insuperable in late old age, when there is no partner, the grown children have moved away, arthritis and breathlessness limit mobility, and life-long friends and relatives have died. Similarly, problems with hearing and sight isolate the individual from other people and all their familiar world. Realistic anxiety can begin to dominate the lives of those elderly people who feel vulnerable: a developing cataract, some deafness and reduced memory for recent events means the boundaries of one's world contract to what one can cope with. Anxiety about running short of money, of being physically attacked, of getting lost, can cause much distress.

Sexual interest and involvement can continue into late old age, with those who have enjoyed a long recurrent sex life usually remaining active for longer than their peers who have not. Even where physical activity is absent, the interest remains to be thought and talked about, for both sexes. Loneliness in old age means not only no sexual intercourse, but a continuing absence of physical contact and tenderness. Such unresolved needs can lead to the sad spectacle of people being labelled as 'dirty old men' (or women). Emotional and sexual bonding – falling in love – can continue to occur well into old age, if the opportunity presents itself.

Emotional health in old age, then, is something which, like physical health, can and should be built on earlier healthy lifestyles. It needs to be maintained by the presence of physical forms of security (e.g. income, personal supports) and by a continuing sense of purposeful participation in the local social world.

SOCIETY'S VIEW OF OLD AGE

In societies where the printed word is rare or non-existent, traditionally the elders have been important as the source of memorised history and knowledge. As older people graduated to less strenuous pursuits they took up the respected and honoured roles of head-men, priests and sages. Modern 'retirement' signifies less activity, but leaves no role at all, let alone one that is valued.

Major technical changes have tended to undermine the previous status of elderly people. As examples: new rapid technological advances have left the skills and knowledge of older people obsolete, as happened in the change from rural to industrial society (Chapter 2) and they are not needed to practise or teach them; increased mobility separates the extended family and undermines their traditional authority; and a mobile society reduces one's value as a *person*, so value much more is dependent on one's *work role*. While this loss in status of the elderly is increasing even in those countries traditionally respectful of age, there are signs in the Western world that the voting and spending powers of increasing numbers of retired people in good health, with no dependants, and with planned pensions, are commanding growing 'respect' from the commercial and political worlds.

But how is old age defined? In some countries, such as India where the average life expectancy is still only 52, some people may be labelled as old in their late forties. Does it start at 60? The biblical life span is 70 (three score years and ten) but many people are now enjoying an active life in their eighties.

It seems that to a considerable extent people begin to *behave* as old, because the calendar, or society, *says* they are getting old, even when their abilities have not greatly changed. (Woman in some Mediterranean countries, for example, especially if widowed, go into black or dreary clothing permanently by their forties.) The expectation of people and society around them, that they will change in function at 'official stages' in life is important and is of special interest in considering the lifetime stories of adults with mental handicap.

Experiences of ordinary life can be grouped throughout in successive stages. There is childhood, where the individual is learning how to function as an independent but social being; adolescence, when the mature adult status is prepared for; young adulthood, when lifestyles and new families are established; middle life, when responsibilities, roles and relationships may alter, increase or decrease; and then retirement. The last of these may be seen as a loss, or as a time to pursue many valuable and enjoyable activities at will. Retired people have a variety of contributions to make in society, including their time, knowledge and the wisdom that can come with a longer perspective of life.

But what about those people with a mental handicap who grow old? What stages of life have they lived out?

OLD AGE AND MENTAL HANDICAP

The old age of people with a mental handicap has not been of any interest until recently. For various reasons there are more people with handicaps who are elderly, especially in the institutions, and this has forced attention on their needs.

Some physical conditions associated with mental handicap are recognised to reduce life expectancy. Thus individuals badly affected by cerebral palsy may develop chronic chest and circulation problems; or severe epilepsy, when difficult to control, may shorten life. Down's syndrome is a condition in which the whole ageing process starts earlier than in most people. The majority of people with Down's syndrome in the past did not reach adult life because of their vulnerability to infections and associated heart and other problems, then untreatable. The majority of adults with mental handicap, however, do not have major physical disabilities which might be expected to shorten their lives, and the improved general health care and nutrition experienced by many adults of the present elderly generation as a whole has presumably enabled more of them to survive for longer. It is important to know if old age is particularly different for people with mental handicap and if it presents any additional needs and problems.

Where are the elderly people with mental handicap? Before the 1950s many young adults were placed in institutions because they troubled society: they had illegitimate babies, or committed minor offences, or had no family; but the common feature was that they were seen as intellectually slow. Thousands of young men and women were sent into institutions over those years and there were enormous and dreadful obstacles to getting out. This is what has created an elderly institutional population 50 years later.

Chapter 10 shows that almost all the practice needed to develop and maintain the skills of *normal* daily life is denied to 'inmates'. The absence of such living skills and the loss of a family home guaranteed a failure to get discharged. Of the adults admitted during that period, those with severe and multiple handicaps did not survive to old age. Their physical ailments (especially before antibiotics and physiotherapy were available) commonly led to relatively early deaths. Those who have survived in the institutions into late old age are therefore very often people with only very mild handicap. During the past 10 years a great many of such able people in middle life have left the institutions for a variety of new homes; it has been difficult for some large rural hospitals, however, to enable this. There are, therefore, several hospitals for the mentally handicapped in the UK where elderly men and women who came in decades back, form a quarter or more of the residential population. Alongside them are people with severe multiple handicaps surviving into late middle age in greater numbers than has previously been known.

Where are the other elderly adults with mental handicap? Since the mid-1960s, adults with a mental handicap who lived in their parents' home have received rather more support to remain there. For example, regular school attendance, day care at ATCs and short-term care have shared some of the responsibility. In addition, their own parents have survived longer and been available to continue the care.

For local authorities, the first awareness of a growing need apparently arose from the necessity to decide whether people attending ATCs should be retired at 60 in order to provide vacancies for the queue of school leavers with mental handicap. The effect of such a retirement was to place the total responsibility for daytime occupation on parents, who could be in their eighties, or on other elderly relatives. It must be remembered that the parents of a 45-year-old person are likely to be 70 plus and where a person with Down's syndrome (now 45) was born to a middle-aged mother, the parents may be 85.

Responses by the local authorities to the existence of middle-aged or older people living with relatives have been generally slow to develop. Some clients will be known because they attend ATC run by the local authority, but those who have never attended and are not outstanding by their behaviour or demands, may remain at home unknown, or at least unserved, and without any plans for their present or future needs.

What actually *are* the needs of older people with mental handicap? Are they special, or any different from those of elderly people generally? By and large we do not know, although some experiences and research may be giving pointers.

First, it must be recognised that the person with a mental handicap has by definition always been a slow learner; for most of those of an earlier generation, that meant any attempts to teach them complex skills were quickly abandoned. Today many more techniques are available. This has left many adults lacking in all sorts of skills, not simply the three Rs, or self-help or domestic abilities, but in the capacity to make choices and in the ability to form mature relationships. It is also very important to understand that not only did others not teach them such skills but they were isolated from an enormous range of situations where they could have taught themselves by watching and experimenting and practising. Isolation from the ordinary learning situations we all use in life could arise from an overprotective environment of the home, or living in the extraordinary environment of an institution. So the person with a mental handicap approaching old age is usually lacking in many skills, and a staggering amount of life experience. People who have to live in environments unsuited to their needs can develop all sorts of survival techniques, and some mentally handicapped people grow up very skilled at getting what they need by 'nuisance' methods. This may be due to being over-indulged and spoiled by parents driven by guilt who find it difficult to say no, or because in an institutional setting they have had to compete for attention.

The response, therefore, of such clients to efforts by others to improve their situation may be one of pleasure and pride, but it may instead be one of resentment. There is inevitably also a varying degree of anxiety ranging from high excitement to outright panic and this anxiety must be recognised and handled sensitively, with both the client and the family.

When then does 'old age' start in people with mental handicap? Four aspects of ageing have already been considered:

physiological, intellectual, emotional and social. These aspects apply equally to those people who are slow learners.

Physiological changes

As already stated the majority of people with severe learning difficulties do not have major life-shortening disabilities: there are innumerable causes of mental handicap, some with physical effects, most without. Down's syndrome has special characteristics which include premature ageing and will be considered under the next heading of Intellectual Changes. Older people who are mentally handicapped are subject to the whole range of medical problems, minor and major, which appear with increasing age: hearing loss (already common in mental handicap), cataracts, overweight, raised blood pressure and heart disease, cancer, arthritis, for example. There has been a tendency until recently for many health problems in later life to be ignored and regarded as an inevitable part of getting old; there is the same approach often in the case of mental handicap, and it is essential that the medical disorders be fully diagnosed and treated, as they are frequently reversible and can certainly always be helped. Physical deterioration should never be accepted simply as due to old age or mental handicap.

Intellectual changes

It is a fact that 95% of the ordinary population are not severely demented even by 75 and even 80% of those over 80 are not severely affected. It is possible that with the exception of one special group (Down's syndrome) older people with mental handicap do not differ from the general population, but it has been recognised for a long time that people with Down's syndrome are very likely to age prematurely in every way including their intellectual functioning.

DEMENTIA

Dementia is the term used for the effects of a chronic (continuing) widespread brain disease, which starts insiduously and is progressive. The person shows increasing intellectual deterioration with a worsening memory for recent events (they have no recollection of breakfast, but may still, and only, vividly recall childhood): they become disorientated in time and space, do not know where they are, or the time, or the day. If these symptoms occur in an individual who is fully conscious, then dementia is the likely diagnosis, but it still cannot be guaranteed without investigation. Such symptoms in a person who is also drowsy, however, suggest other emergency conditions, such as tumour, head injury or delirium. Dementia eventually erodes personality as well as intellect, and destroys relationships. Severe dementia is devastating: 'the true self dies long before the body's death. In the intervening years a smudged caricature disintegrates noisily, and without dignity into chaos' (Pitt, 1982).

There are two main forms of dementia, one known as Alzheimer's disease (AD), named after the man who originally described it in 1907, and a second form due to the various effects of hardening of the arteries (arteriosclerosis) in the brain. There are similar changes in mental functioning in this latter variety, but whereas in AD the deterioration is a continuous slide, in arteriosclerosis dementia the deterioration, which may include little strokes, blackouts, or occasional fits, tends to go downhill in steps and the effects are patchy. The symptoms and signs of AD reflect the damage occurring in the various parts of the brain which have special functions. Increasing forgetfulness has already been mentioned; this starts with recent events, although distant memory may remain much longer and the person may behave as though they know only their past, for example searching for their mother but not recognising their own children. The memory loss includes such things as where they are, in time as well as space. This disorientation can lead to an inability to remember where the toilet is: this is distressing and contributes to incontinence. Finally, the individual not only cannot remember or recognise family members, but does not even remember who and what she herself is. That is a final and total disintegration of a personality.

As forgetfulness increases there is also difficulty in finding the right words, and understanding what is said; problems in organising movements in space eventually affect such acts as dressing and feeding. Interest in life dwindles and the individual becomes apathetic; judgement and insight go. For a while self-awareness of the problem may be kept at bay by denying the memory loss and concocting stories to cover up, by blaming others for things being apparently lost. Emotionally the person can become very labile, moving from tears to laughter to anger, speedily and often without apparent cause. The mixture of apathy, forgetfulness and other problems leads to a state of messiness with food, clothing and hygiene. A person with severe dementia is liable to wander off anywhere and get lost, or interfere with gas or electrical appliances with no awareness of danger. The personality may totally change, with a once warm natured individual becoming relentlessly hostile and even violent towards their loving relatives, with deeply distressing effects. The total process may cover several years, but once the individual is severely demented he seldom survives more than about two years. Women tend to outnumber men with this disorder.

The Alzheimer variety of dementia is a *disease* and not simply due to ageing. Because there are many more very elderly people in the population now, and 20% of the over-eighties show some dementia, the problems presented by this disorder have attracted mounting scientific attention. As noted earlier, people with Down's syndrome have long been recognised as being prone to age prematurely and to develop Alzheimer's disease, quite commonly by 50. (When dementia due to any cause appears before the age of 65 it is labelled *pre-senile* dementia.) Research into the nature of Down's syndrome has now been linked to research of

Alzheimer's disease and the genetic and other factors they may have in common. It is known, for example, that in Alzheimer's disease there is a deficiency of a certain chemical transmitter (acetylcholine) in particular parts of the brain. In Parkinson's disease, (the 'Shaking Palsy') a different chemical transmitter (L-dopa) is deficient in the special focal area and the improvements in that condition which can occur by giving L-dopa, gives hope that Alzheimer's might one day be helped by comparable means.

Far more common than actual dementia in elderly people is *depression*, which can present the same picture as dementia and is then sometimes called pseudo-dementia. For a variety of reasons a depressive state might quietly develop: the individual may gradually become apathetic, forgetful, self-neglectful, irritable, possibly aggressive, incontinent, sleepless and wandering at night. They, of course, appear to be dementing. It is crucial for the depression to be diagnosed, as it is both treatable and reversible, unlike true dementia. Just to make the problem more complex and to highlight the importance of careful diagnosis, an individual in the early phases of true dementia may realise what is happening and become very depressed as a result. Their psychiatric management will have to include both aspects, of course. The Alzheimer variety of dementia is the commonest one but there are various biochemical disorders, usually hormone or vitamin deficiencies (but occasionally chronic chemical poisoning, e.g. lead) which can, over a period of time, reduce the overall functioning of the brain.

In investigating individuals (which can also include middle-aged people, who appear to be dementing) many such possibilities must be eliminated. Vitamin deficiencies arising from chronic alcoholism, or faddy diets, or even prolonged drug use; and the thyroid gland's underactivity are important examples. All of them can seriously and even permanently reduce mental functioning. Under-functioning of the thyroid (hypothyroidism) becomes more common with age in many people. A severe degree of its results in mental and physical functioning being slowed almost to a stop with obesity, facial coarseness and growling voice, swollen legs and a perpetual experience of coldness. Thyroid functioning, however, can become quite reduced without the physical signs being too obvious and it may be the mental deterioration which presents first. Treatment with thyroxine usually improves the mental state along with the other symptoms, but if the condition has been unrecognised for a long time the outlook is much poorer. Yet again this is another condition with particular relevance to people with Down's syndrome who are especially prone to develop thyroid disorders, usually a deficiency, but occasionally an excess of its activity.

Emotional changes

Reference was made earlier to the rope or plait of various changing careers throughout the length of ordinary people's lives, and the usual phases of adulthood and their changing responsibilities and experiences. Adults with mental handicap have, as they grow older, a rope of life which is usually thin and impoverished. Their parents experienced much rejection by society, a great sense of guilt about their child's condition, and no skilled advice (there was none available then). The parents recognised that society did not want their child, and that they carried the responsibility quite alone.

Although social attitudes in the West have changed considerably since then, some parents have never lost that sense of total responsibility, so even denying any to the person with the disability himself. In shouldering the responsibility of permanent parenting, they of course expect that their son or daughter will retain the permanent role of child. Because until now society has expected parents to provide a place in their home indefinitely (until a crisis occurs), the adult who is intellectually disabled has remained a guest in the house of the previous generation, even if he has escaped the 'child' role, and both generations have had to make big sacrifices as a result.

For some, of course, the parental home could not remain

their home, and those individuals became inmates of institutions (as described in Chapter 10) and in doing so suffered
often a triple bereavement: the loss of parents, the loss of home
and all its associations, and the loss of their individuality to the
corporate institutional lifestyle. The emotional development of
such adults can present some differences from those who
remain with relatives, and will be discussed later.

Previous generations of parents with a disabled son or daughter had to develop a degree of resignation both towards society's
attitude and to the bleak future. There was certainly no expectation of marriage, parenthood, or householder status for their
child, and, indeed, the whole expectation was that of perpetual
childhood – the Peter Pan Syndrome – (he never grew up). The
young disabled adult remained in permanent proximity to the
parents, and this showed effects in a number of ways.

A very obvious one, even at a distance, is the style of dress.
The 25-year-old daughter may be dressed in skirts and socks
like a 10-year-old, or at 35 may be dressed like 35-year-olds *in
mother's day*. By the time mother is in her seventies, it is likely
that she and her daughter of 50 wear similar 'elderly' clothes.
That daughter, while in the fashion sense is passing vaguely
from a prolonged childish style into a permanent and outdated
middle-aged style, is likely to have a sense of personal identity
similarly lacking the phases of life which adults normally experience in their 'rope of careers'.

Does the adult with a mental handicap who has led such an
unvarying life since youth perceive himself, or expect to be, any
different at 50 from what he was at 30? Certainly, people who
have spent their lives in institutions have been shown often to
have little awareness of the phases of life, or their own age.
Adults who have remained at home have in some studies shown
that they are aware of the passing of time, but more in relation
to their parents' growing frailties, than in viewing their own
approaching old age.

The practical and emotional barriers to going anywhere
without their handicapped child, which were experienced long

ago by the parents, continue to produce a variety of effects. First, the parents themselves are unable to separate from their grown-up 'child', and so remain limited in their own personal developments. Second, the son or daughter takes on a permanently dependent role (and not just physically), and this can result in their coming to exploit the parents, or to a sense of guilt at being a burden, or to a situation of unresolved conflict where the offspring tries unsuccessfully to stop the parental management of their lives. All these experiences, and especially all the *missing* experiences, contribute to the impoverished 'rope of careers' of the older person with a mental handicap.

Perhaps the biggest deficit in the personal development of most intellectually disabled people is in the field of social and relationship skills. Loneliness is usually a major problem in their lives, but finding 'a friend' for them is not the total answer. *Having* a friend is not the same as *being* a friend: this involves a two-way process which does not develop naturally in people who have become used only to *taking* what *others give*. Learning to build and sustain such two-way relationships involving consideration of each other's feelings and wishes, takes skilled guidance and opportunities. This is a life experience to be undertaken from childhood onwards, and many people of normal intelligence find it very difficult to catch up later.

REFERENCE

Pitt, B. (1982). *Psycho-geriatrics. An Introduction to the Psychiatry of Old Age*, 2nd edition, p. 39. Churchill Livingstone, Edinburgh.

FURTHER READING

Carver, V. and Liddiard, P. (1978). *An Ageing Population*. Hodder and Stoughton, London with Open University Press.

They Never Asked for Help (1980). A study on the needs of elderly retarded people in metro-Toronto sponsored by Help the Aged in co-operation with Metropolitan Toronto Association for the Mentally Retarded.

Chapter 16

Biomedical Causation

It is natural not only for parents, but also others to ask why a person should be significantly intellectually impaired. While such a question may be expected and, of course, reasonable it is regrettable that in many instances it is not possible to provide an answer.

In a number of studies, particularly those of Swedish origin, a careful study of causes has been made, but even with these there are at least 20 per cent in whom no aetiology (definite cause) can be reliably ascribed. From the experience of clinical practice elsewhere it may be felt that our Swedish colleagues are over-optimistic in the description of percentages of persons in whom causes can be reliably suggested. This proportion can be debated endlessly and the figure agreed upon will in part be dependent on the scepticism of the investigators and the extent to which they are able or willing to institute tests or investigations to identify causes or causation. Many feel that in only half of those with a severe intellectual impairment can a cause be identified and in those with mild or moderate impairment the figure is even lower.

Whatever figure is agreed upon it still means that there are families in whom 'the reason why' is unknown and this itself demands care and support in counselling, in which the question of 'guilt' or 'blame' cannot be avoided – illogical though this may seem.

What do we know about causation?

It is easier to consider this question in the context of those who have a severe impairment. By doing so we can make some, but only some, assumptions about causation in the mildly or moderately impaired. In many developed and also developing societies the mildly intellectually impaired can and are absorbed into the society and their identification is thus more difficult. Advances in social facilities and attitudes have for the most part opened up opportunities for more direct integration and contribution as ordinary society members. But what is generally known and acknowledged is that there is within this group (if there really is a group) some social bias grouping towards the lower socio-economic groups with parents perhaps not being so dissimilar in intellectual capacity. This would not appear to be the case with those who are more severely impaired.

It is with this latter group that we are, therefore, led towards supposing that there is impairment of a more 'organic' nature. There is something structurally and functionally abnormal with their brains.

How common is intellectual impairment?

While estimates of frequency for severe intellectual impairment are difficult, those for mild or moderate impairment are even more so. The reasons for this should at least be apparent from what has already been stated.

If European studies are combined and as much as possible made comparable, the figure for severe intellectual impairment is something of the order of 3–4:1000 live births. But such a figure as this will depend upon which population is being surveyed and at what age. There is a significant mortality among the severely intellectually impaired and, although it may seem surprising, some with severe intellectual impairment are not recognised as such (or reported) until they are over a certain age – as late as school entry, or later in some.

Figures for mildly or moderate intellectually impaired persons are notoriously difficult to determine. A consensus view, however, would seem to be that the figure is higher than for severe impairment, but how much higher is difficult to determine. In Sweden the figure is not that much higher than for severe impairment, but elsewhere it may be 4–10 times higher.

CAUSES

A great number of identified (or strongly suspected) causes of severe intellectual impairment are pre-natal (before birth) or peri-natal (at or around the time of birth) although it is at times difficult to tell what is truly pre-natal and what is peri-natal. While estimates vary these two together constitute approximately 75 to 85 per cent of known causes with the pre-natal being of early origin – genetic or chromosomal.

Genetic or chromosomal causes

As many as 30–40 per cent of patients with severe intellectual impairment may have a chromosome abnormality or a defect of a single gene.

With defects of chromosomes many genes are involved and there will be a cluster of abnormalities found in an affected individual. Chromosome abnormalities account for about 30 per cent of those with a severe intellectual impairment; Down's syndrome is the commonest of these.

In the majority of persons with Down's syndrome the abnormality is due to a so-called 'non-disjunction' which produces an extra chromosome on the 21 pair. It is for this reason that it is sometimes referred to as trisomy 21 and the total chromosome count is 47 rather than the normal 46. This form of Down's syndrome increases in incidence in mothers over the age of 35, although the majority are, and have been for many years, born to mothers below this age.

In a very small proportion of persons (2 per cent) with Down's syndrome the abnormality of chromosomes is due to a so-called 'translocation'. The total chromosome count here is 46 as in other individuals. There is no association of this abnormality with increasing maternal age but in 25 per cent of such children the parents will have similar but 'balanced' abnormalities and be normal.

Abnormalities of the sex chromosomes (X or Y) constitute a very small proportion of the total chromosome defects that give rise to severe intellectual impairment. The figure is probably no more than 1 per cent. The presence of an extra X chromosome is closely linked with intellectual impairment and increasingly so with a greater number of abnormal X chromosomes. Attention in recent times has been focused on the so-called fragile X abnormality. It has been suggested that in a male population this abnormality may account for up to 10 per cent of severely intellectually impaired individuals. But the situation is complicated by the fact that this abnormality can be found in normal males and females.

Abnormalities of a single gene probably contribute to 10 per cent of the causes of severe intellectual impairment. Identification of such abnormalities depends on careful examination of the patient, the taking of a family history and in some the institution of relevant biochemical investigations.

Structural disorders of the central nervous system

Hydrocephalus (water on the brain) associated both with spina bifida (the severe structural abnormality of the spine) and sometimes following severe infection of the nervous system or brain haemorrhage, is associated with intellectual impairment. There are other abnormalities of the central nervous system which are of very early pre-natal origin which may be associated with severe intellectual impairment such as encephaloceles, and partial or complete absence of the part of the brain known as the corpus callosum.

Microcephaly is the term used for a small head when this is significantly below the normal size. It may be present in association with other abnormalities (see below) or by itself. In some, microcephaly may be secondary to some infection during pregnancy or it may be of genetic origin. It is invariably associated with some intellectual impairment.

Structural disorders of the central nervous system with multiple 'dysmorphic' features

Structural developmental anomalies of the brain may be inferred through the observations of signs or stigmata that taken together may suggest a specific diagnosis or dysmorphic syndrome. In many, intellectual impairment may be reasonably expected if it has not already been recognised. The number of such syndromes is extremely large and numbers many hundreds. In only 60 per cent of individuals demonstrating multiple abnormalities, including intellectual impairment, will a definite name or diagnosis be ascribed. In those that are, 10 per cent may have a definite genetic basis.

The clinical features of these syndromes are various and most clinicians depend on the employment of an atlas to identify individuals because although they may be great in number they are individually rare. One of the most well-known of the atlases is *Recognisable Patterns of Human Malformation* by David Smith.

Some examples of such syndromes are given below:

LAURENCE–MOON–BIEDL SYNDROME

The principal features of this rare 'recessively' inherited condition are severe intellectual impairment, retinitis pigmentosa (degeneration of the retina of the eye), obesity, small genitalia and polydactyly (increased numbers of fingers or toes). There is a further strong association with deafness and with heart disease. The diagnosis is easy if all five cardinal features are present, but it is agreed that the syndrome may exist when only two or three features are present and also that it can exist with other features such as optic atrophy (deterioration of the optic nerve) rather than retinitis pigmentosa.

Diagnosis is important because of the genetic (25 per cent chance of recurrence) and prognostic implications.

INCONTINENTIA PIGMENTI (BLOCH-SULZBERGER DISEASE)

This disorder may be X-linked and in the affected males lethal at birth so that only heterozygote (carrier) females survive. The diagnosis of incontinentia pigmenti is based on characteristic skin lesions in a girl, which may be present from infancy. From an initial inflammatory or vesicular (like chickenpox) type of skin lesion the progression is towards pigmentation over large areas of the body. A third of such children are severely intellectually impaired and an equal proportion have delayed intellectual development. Alopecia (loss of hair), various eye abnormalities and skeletal abnormalities are common.

As the condition may be X-linked it has been suggested that mothers of affected children should be carefully examined for any minor skin manifestation of the disorder.

APERT'S SYNDROME (ACROCEPHALOSYNDACTYLY)

The principal features of this rare disorder are that affected children have short but high heads, prominent eyes and varying degrees of syndactyly (joining together of the fingers or toes).

Intellectual impairment is common, but not invariably associated and the severity may not be marked.

The genetic pattern is autosomal dominant (50 per cent chance of recurrence), although the majority occur as fresh mutations. An association between this condition and a high paternal age has been suggested.

SMITH–LEMLI–OPITZ SYNDROME

This rare autosomal recessive disorder is invariably associated with intellectual impairment and often with poor growth, floppiness of muscle, microcephaly with a narrow frontal area, ptosis (drooping of the eyelids), and slanting or low-set ears. A single palmar (simian) skin crease is common and cryptorchidism (small or absent testes) and other genital abnormalities are often seen in the male. Several other associations have also been reported which include seizures, heart defects, cataracts and syndactyly of the second and third toes. The diagnosis is more commonly made in males, probably because of the genital abnormalities. There is a 25 per cent chance of recurrence in a brother or sister.

RILEY–DAY SYNDROME (FAMILIAL DYSAUTONOMIA)

There are many clinical features in the Riley–Day syndrome indicative of autonomic nervous system dysfunction (the nervous system that controls heart rate, body temperature and the movement of the gut).

Half the affected individuals are intellectually impaired and half have epilepsy. Infants do not thrive. Swallowing difficulties, aspiration pneumonias and cyclical vomiting are common.

The most well-known clinical features in the Riley–Day syndrome are due to the autonomic dysfunction: abnormal sweating, skin blotching, insensitivity to pain, lack of tear formation (severe enough to cause scarring of the cornea), taste deficiency, unstable temperature, labile blood pressure, urinary frequency and absent tendon reflexes.

The aspiration pneumonia and cardiac disorders pose a serious threat to survival and many children die before the age of 10.

The genetic pattern is that of an autosomal recessive condition and the condition is more common in Ashkenazim Jews.

SOTOS SYNDROME (CEREBRAL GIGANTISM)

It is not known why children with Sotos syndrome have such rapid growth and doubt exists as to whether all of those diagnosed as having this syndrome do really have a single specific aetiology. Over 80 per cent are intellectually impaired.

Children with Sotos syndrome are large at birth with particularly large heads and feet. There is a prominent forehead (dolichocephaly), downward-slanting eyes, hypertelorism (widely-spaced eyes), a large chin, a high palate and coarse facial features.

Growth rate in the early years is excessive but slows down later, resulting in a near normal adult height.

This is not a genetically determined disorder.

NEUROCUTANEOUS SYNDROMES (PHAKOMATOSES)

Several disorders are commonly recognised as coming under this general heading including tuberose sclerosis, neurofribromatosis, the Sturge–Weber syndrome, von Hippel–Lindau syndrome and ataxia telangiectasia. The unifying features are that they all have some disorder of the nervous system and the skin.

TUBEROUS SCLEROSIS (EPILOIA, ADENOMA SEBACEUM OR BOURNVILLE'S DISEASE)

This is a neurocutaneous syndrome that should not escape mention because of its high association with intellectual impairment (and epilepsy).

Tuberose sclerosis is a 'dominantly' inherited condition with widely-varying penetrance (severity) and a 'high mutation' rate.

There is a classical triad of epilepsy, intellectual impairment and skin lesions, although only 40 per cent ultimately have the usual skin features, and only 60 per cent are intellectually impaired, but most have epilepsy.

A high index of suspicion should exist in children or adults who are intellectually impaired and have epilepsy, particularly if the latter is of the early onset infantile spasms variety. Skin lesions may be difficult to detect in an infant, as they may consist only of small pale patches best seen under ultraviolet light using a Wood's filter.

Following diagnosis, parents should be examined in order to offer reliable genetic advice, i.e. has there been a 'mutation' or is there a dominant inheritance from one of them?

VON RECKLINGHAUSEN'S DISEASE (NEUROFRIBROMATOSIS)

Small cutaneous (skin) tumours and numerous flat café-au-lait skin patches are the diagnostic features of this condition. A variety of tumours may occur in other tissues or organs – in the central or peripheral nervous system, bones, muscles and endocrine glands.

The tumours that may be seen in the skin are neurofribromata and are related to nerves. Besides the tumours in the cutaneous nerves, there appears to be a tendency towards similar growth in the optic and the auditory nerves and the meninges (coverings) of the brain and spinal cord. In some, the principal clinical findings will be the café-au-lait patches that appear in early infancy while in others the two features, the patches and the cutaneous tumours, co-exist.

Various abnormalities are associated with von Recklinghausen's disease: hypertrophy (overgrowth) of extremities or parts of the body may occur, malignant (cancerous) changes, a variety of bone abnormalities, endocrine abnormalities and also tumours of the medulla of the adrenal glands – phaeochromocytoma.

About half the people with von Recklinghausen's disease may develop some neurological symptom and between 5 and 10 per cent may develop malignant disease.

Intellectual impairment is three times as common as in the general population although the reason for this is not fully understood. Seizures occur frequently and may be associated with a brain tumour. A parent will often have some of the features of von Recklinhausen's disease.

STURGE–WEBER SYNDROME

A cutaneous haemangioma (port wine stain) of one side of the face, commonly associated with a hemiplegia on the other side, intellectual impairment and epilepsy are all hallmarks of the Sturge–Weber syndrome. In some the skin lesions may be more extensive. Buphthalmos (bull's eye), which is an intense increase in pressure of the eye at or near to birth due to lack of drainage of fluid from inside the eye, is also associated with this syndrome. On the same side as the facial skin lesions, there will be an abnormal development of the blood vessels on the surface of the brain particularly in the so-called occipital and parietal areas – leptomeningeal angiomatosis. Calcium will be deposited in these abnormal vessels and sometimes show up on the radiographs of the skull with a characteristic 'railroad track' appearance of double contour lines.

Of patients with Sturge–Weber syndrome 90 per cent have epilepsy, 30 per cent are intellectually impaired and 30–40 per cent have a hemiplegia on the side opposite to the haemangioma. Control of the epilepsy may be difficult and at times hemispherectomy (removal of half of the brain) has to be undertaken.

The Sturge–Weber syndrome is not genetically determined.

Toxic substances

A number of maternally ingested drugs may have an adverse affect upon fetal development.

ALCOHOL

It has been suggested that maternally ingested alcohol may be the third commonest known cause of intellectual impairment after Down's syndrome and the neural tube defects – and the most preventable. The term 'fetal alcohol syndrome' has been coined for the association between dysmorphic features, poor fetal growth and various neurodevelopmental abnormalities.

Alcohol ingestion in the early weeks of pregnancy appears to pose the greatest risk.

MATERNAL PHENYLKETONURIA

Untreated maternal phenylketonuria (an inherited abnormality of amino acids) during pregnancy may be associated with microcephaly and other physical and developmental abnormalities.

An infection in the mother may be passed to the fetus. Such intra-uterine infections may occur from a variety of different organisms and cause severe defects within the developing nervous system as well as other body systems. Pre-eminent among the group are the organisms toxoplasma, rubella, cytomegalovirus (CMV) and herpes simplex. Together they are often nicknamed 'TORCH infections.

Toxoplasmosis: While many of the population – up to 60 per cent in Britain – have at some time been infected by the protozoan organism, *Toxoplasma gondii*, its principal significance is for the most part when it infects, for the first time, a woman while pregnant. The organism may cross the placenta. In 45 per cent of cases infection of the fetus may occur, the possibility increasing throughout the duration of pregnancy.

The stigmata of congenital toxoplasmosis will include chorioretinitis (an inflammation and scarring of part of the retina), microcephaly or calcification in the brain. Other more widespread signs of infection occur – jaundice and hepatosplenomegaly (enlargement of the liver and spleen). But only 10 to 20 per cent of congenitally affected infants have clinically apparent signs at birth. The signs of neurological damage may only appear months or even years later.

Cytomegalovirus (CMV): CMV alone may account for up to 10 per cent of known cases of intellectual impairment. The major risk to the fetus is when the primary maternal infection occurs during pregnancy as distinct from a reactivation occurring from a previous infection. Only about 20 per cent of mothers are symptomatic when infected. When a primary infection occurs during pregnancy it is likely that 5 per cent of fetuses will be affected. The vast majority of affected infants will be asymptomatic at the time of birth.

Post-natally, microcephaly with calcification in the brain may be noted together with the early onset of seizures.

Congenital rubella (German measles): Due partly to active immunisation programmes in Britain for schoolgirls the incidence of congenital rubella has significantly declined, although some slight increase has been noted in recent times because of incomplete immunisation uptake.

In those women in whom rubella during pregnancy is symptomatic there is approximately a 50 per cent risk to the fetus,' when asymptomatic the risk is considerably lower, about 20 per cent. The state of gestation will also determine the risks to the fetus in terms of severity as a result of being infected. If maternal infection occurs during the first 12 weeks the risk might be as high as 80 per cent and as low as 25 per cent by the end of the second trimester (third).

It is important to recognise that prolonged follow-up after birth is necessary if congenital rubella infection is suspected, as deafness might be the only finding not apparent until later infancy.

Herpes simplex: Neonatal herpes simplex infection, in the majority, is acquired during passage through an infected birth canal. Less commonly, transplacental passage of virus causes intra-uterine infection. Unlike cytomegalovirus infection virtually all examples of neonatal herpes simplex infections are symptomatic often with serious neurological concomitants apparent in the newborn period.

Peri-natal causes

A number of peri-natal (within the first week of life) problems may ultimately give rise to an intellectual impairment. Most usually, however, there will be accompanying significant physical abnormalities, for example, cerebral palsy.

The risks of major developmental problems are far higher in the small, whether premature or light-for-dates, baby. Particular problems are posed by the very low birth-weight baby (under 1500g birth-weight). With an immaturity of the respiratory system in such small infants, impairment of oxygen supply to the brain may cause lasting damage.

Biochemical disorders (including inborn errors of metabolism)

There are several transitory biochemical abnormalities that can occur in the newly-born baby – particularly the premature or light-for-dates baby. These will include low blood sugar (hypoglycaemia), abnormalities of the level of calcium (hypocalcaemia) and a number of other biochemical abnormalities. Early recognition of these abnormalities and appropriate treatment is not usually associated with any lasting developmental problems. A failure to do this can result in an infant having a major developmental problem.

In addition to the relatively common biochemical abnormalities referred to above there are some less common situations in which a biochemical abnormality is as a result of an inherited inborn error of metabolism. In such situations as these there is most usually a missing enzyme.

The most well described so-called inborn error of metabolism, is *phenylketonuria*. In this condition an abnormal level of the chemical phenylalanine occurs. In the United Kingdom the condition is automatically screened for in the first few days of life and, when it is identified, dietary treatment in the first few years of life is accompanied by normal development. A failure to diagnose phenylketonuria will mean that in most children there will be major developmental problems accompanied by epilepsy.

Galactosaemia is an inherited abnormality of carbohydrate metabolism. If not recognised an infant will have jaundice, develop cataracts and have severe intellectual impairment. The recognition of this disorder in the newborn period and the removal of lactose from the diet is most usually associated with subsequent normal development.

Besides the two examples already mentioned large numbers

of other similar but less common inherited biochemical abnormalities exist. Some are amenable to principally dietary treatment but others not.

In some, extremely rare, situations progressive degenerative disorders of the nervous system occur due to an abnormal storage of a material in the central nervous system due again to a missing enzyme. Many biochemical abnormalities can now be diagnosed in the fetus by means of amniocentesis (aspiration of fluid from the womb) and is a form of examination that may be offered when there is a high risk of the baby's having such a disorder, for example the birth of a child already with a biochemical abnormality.

Underactivity of the thyroid gland (hypothyroidism) has now been recognised as being common. Treatment instituted as soon as possible after birth is thought to be accompanied by normal or near-normal development. Failure to treat or to institute early treatment is typically associated with major developmental abnormalities and growth impairment – cretinism. In the United Kingdom hypothyroidism is now screened for in the same way as phenylketonuria.

Post-natal causes

Infection of the central nervous system in early infancy is often associated with subsequent intellectual impairment. Mortality with neonatal (in the first month of life) meningitis may be between 30 and 80 per cent and of those that survive 20 to 50 per cent will have severe damage to the nervous system.

Severe encephalitis (inflammation of the brain) particularly with the virus herpes simplex is associated with a high mortality but equally so with a very high morbidity and subsequent intellectual impairment, often with epilepsy.

Head injuries are more common in children than adults and a significant minority sustain a permanent neurological deficit. Head injuries in children are frequently due to road traffic accidents whether the child is a pedestrian or a cyclist.

Non-accidental injury to children may often include head trauma, either by direct blows to the head or secondary to severe shaking. In a number the end result may be cerebral palsy with associated intellectual impairment.

Severe head injury at any age can result in significant intellectual and physical impairments. In developing and developed countries one of the commonest causes of severe head injuries is due to traffic accidents. The introduction of seat belt legislation in some countries has resulted in a significant decrease of such injuries.

In some areas and in some countries drowning is a common accident. Near-drowning is a term given to those who are rescued from water in an unconscious state. While figures do vary it is argued by many that near-drowning can be a cause of brain damage in both children and adults.

The effect of ageing on individuals may be associated with intellectual impairment. In some there may be a specific disease process present which may be as varied as a brain tumour, a so-called slow virus infection or pre-senile dementias, the causes of which have still to be determined.

This chapter has attempted to indicate the variety of biomedical causes that exist for a person being intellectually impaired. It has inevitably concentrated on those causes that are of congenital or early onset. It is important, however, to bear in mind, as emphasised at the beginning of the chapter, that there is a great deal still that is not known in relation to the biomedical causation of severe (and mild) intellectual impairment. Much research is still needed.

FURTHER READING

Dobbing, J. (ed.) (1984). *Scientific Studies in Mental Retardation*. The Royal Society of Medicine with Macmillan Press Limited, London.
Hagberg, B. (1978). The epidemiological panorama of major neuropaediatric handicaps in Sweden. In *Care of the Handicapped Child*,

pp. 111–24 (ed. Apley, J.). Spastics International Medical Publications with William Heinemann Medical Books, London.

Smith, D. W. (1982). *Recognizable Patterns of Human Malformations: Genetic, Embryologic and Clinical Aspects*, 3rd edition. (Volume 7 of Major Problems in Clinical Practice series.) W. B. Saunders Co, Philadelphia.

Chapter 17

Commonly Associated Disorders: Epilepsy and Cerebral Palsy

EPILEPSY

Epilepsy is probably the commonest medical problem that occurs in severely intellectually impaired persons. Estimates inevitably vary but probably up to 30 per cent have one or other form of epilepsy; in many this will start in infancy and the form of epilepsy will often be complex and severe. Even those with Down's syndrome, in whom it is often stated that epilepsy is rare, this may only be so when compared to others with similar intellectual impairment. It is still much more common than in the general population. As a generalisation it can be stated that the more severe the intellectual impairment, the greater the chances of a person having epilepsy.

What is epilepsy?

Epilepsy is not a specific disease, but a state where there is a transitory disturbance of brain function of a recurrent nature. Hughlings Jackson described the individual disturbance or seizure as an 'excessive neuronal discharge' and the later development of electroencephalography (EEG) in the 1920s and 1930s has supported this earlier suggestion. The underlying mechanisms that relate to the production of such excessive neuronal discharges are still poorly understood.

Classification

There are many different types of epilepsy and their classification is a subject of continuous debate. They can be grouped into partial and generalised epilepsies with the cause being known in some which are, therefore, referred to as 'symptomatic'; but in the majority a cause is not identified and they are thus referred to as 'idiopathic'. The partial epilepsies include Jacksonian focal epilepsies and some psychomotor or temporal lobe epilepsies (see below). The generalised epilepsies include petit mal, tonic clonic (grand mal), atonic, akinetic (drop attacks), generalised myoclonic, and infantile spasms. Consciousness is always impaired in generalised but not necessarily in the partial epilepsies.

Diagnosis

The diagnosis of epilepsy may be difficult and mistakes occur. The number of alternative diagnoses is wide and will include hypoglycaemia (a low blood sugar), habit spasms or tics, breath-holding attacks in young children, migraine, paroxysmal vertigo, syncope (fainting), tetany, and simulated seizures or 'pseudo-epilepsy'.

The diagnosis depends almost entirely on a clear description of the attack from any eye witnesses and in many cases the person himself. Diagnosis is difficult without an eye-witness account. It is necessary to know the frequency, duration, exact character, timing and precipitating factors of an attack. In addition it is important to ascertain whether there has been any aura or warning of an impending attack and to know the state of the person immediately after the episode.

A general and neurological examination should be undertaken by a doctor of any person who may have had an epileptic seizure.

Investigations and tests

The role of specialist investigations and tests in confirming the diagnosis of epilepsy is controversial. But such tests may define what form of epilepsy is present and also determine the aetiology or causation. They are not substitutes for obtaining a clear description of the attack.

A skull radiograph may be normal in most, although occasionally small areas of calcium may be seen which can be diagnostically helpful. More detailed radiological studies such as computerised axial tomography (CT scan) are undertaken when there is an appropriate indication to do so.

Electroencephalography (EEG) is often undertaken in persons who may have had an epileptic seizure. However, it is known that persons who have had definite seizures have also had normal EEG records at the time the studies were carried out and, conversely, some who have not had seizures appear to have records suggestive of an epileptic disturbance.

In persons with severe intellectual impairment abnormal EEGs are very common whether they do or do not have epilepsy. This is, nevertheless, a non-invasive investigation (i.e. no x-rays or injections) and one for which only limited cooperation is necessary. An EEG can assist in deciding which form of epilepsy exists.

More recently it has become possible to record the EEG over prolonged periods of time – for 24 hours or longer. This is known as ambulatory EEG. The electrodes are attached to the skull in the usual way and the person wears a small recorder on the body that can continue to record for at least 24 hours.

Biochemical investigations are sometimes appropriate. These may be quite simple, such as the measurement of the blood sugar, or complex when there is a suspicion that a metabolic disorder may exist.

Seizures or epilepsy in children

There are several forms of epilepsy that occur in children but are less commonly seen in adults, and even within infancy and childhood there are specific forms that occur at one age and not another.

THE NEONATAL PERIOD

Seizures are common in the neonatal period (the first month of life), but because of their uncharacteristic presentation they are difficult to recognise. It can at times be very difficult to differentiate seizures from paroxysmal changes in behaviour in many newborn infants. Some forms of seizure in the neonate will be seen in the premature but not in the full-term infant. In some varieties, such as the clonic seizures, the cause may be something as simple as hypoglycaemia (a low blood sugar) or hypocalcaemia (low calcium), or alternatively be indicative of definite brain injury. The same has to be said about other definite seizures that can occur at this time of life.

LATER INFANCY

Infantile spasms: The infantile spasms syndrome is a severe form of epilepsy which has a specific age of onset, most typically between the ages of 5 and 13 months. The infantile spasms syndrome by popular acceptance refers to a combination of typically sudden flexor spasms of the whole body (they can less commonly be extensor or confined to one part of the body) associated usually with regression of development and an abnormal EEG. The EEG very commonly has an abnormality referred to as 'hypsarrhythmia'.

Infantile spasms are usually considered in two major groups. In the one group there are children with an already recognised anomaly or retarded development – *symptomatic type*, while in the other the development of spasms occurs in a previously well infant with no evidence of brain damage – the *cryptogenic type*. It is not always possible to place a child in one or other group, although an attempt to do so is important for prognostic reasons.

Two-thirds of the patients with a diagnosis of infantile

spasms will fit into the symptomatic group, although the exact cause remains unknown in at least half. The causes that might be identified include tuberose sclerosis (in approximately 25 per cent of cases) (Chapter 16), congenital infections of the central nervous system, some metabolic disorders and a variety of brain malformations which may range from trisomy 21 (Down's syndrome) through to major structural abnormalities of the brain (Chapter 16).

The outlook for intellectual development and long-term freedom from seizures is poor. Fifty per cent of the children with cryptogenic spasms have continuing problems with delayed intellectual development and seizures, whereas in the symptomatic group the outlook is worse, i.e. 80 per cent have delayed intellectual development and seizures.

LATER CHILDHOOD

Tonic-clonic seizures (grand mal): This is one of the commonest seizure disorders in childhood, adolescence and adulthood.

A good eye-witness account of a tonic-clonic seizure should leave little diagnostic doubt. Tonic-clonic seizures consist of a loss of consciousness and posture, stiffening (tonic phase), generalised jerking movements (clonic phase), facial flushing, incontinence, tongue biting, salivation from the mouth, and if the seizures are in any way prolonged, there will be some cyanosis (blueness due to lack of oxygen). After an attack many will have a headache and be sleepy. Amnesia for the event is usual. Careful clinical examination is mandatory and may be supplemented by plain skull radiographs and later an EEG. In a high proportion of people with tonic-clonic seizures, particularly children, even with a careful history, clinical examination and investigations, a cause will not be identified.

Petit mal seizures: This term is all too frequently used loosely to describe all forms of 'absence' attacks. Petit mal attacks, which are relatively uncommon, usually start between 5 and 12 years. They consist of momentary cessation of activity and awareness, and are normally associated with a characteristic EEG abnormality – 3Hz (cycles per second) spike and wave formation. Although the individual attacks last only a few seconds they may be frequent and interfere with school work. Some flickering of the eyes is sometimes seen but there is never any falling. Attacks may be precipitated by overbreathing. Petit mal seizures are more common in girls, and carry a generally favourable prognosis.

Psychomotor or temporal lobe attacks: Temporal lobe epilepsy may be caused by prolonged fever-associated seizures in early childhood because of scarring of the temporal lobe of the brain. Small congenital tumours can sometimes also be the cause of this form of epilepsy. In a small proportion of patients this form of epilepsy may be inherited. In most no cause is identified.

Temporal lobe or psychomotor epilepsy may be difficult to distinguish from petit mal attacks. Common presentations are with altered sensations and awareness, and vacancy. These altered sensations (aura) can either be an abnormal taste in the mouth, a feeling of 'having been here before' (déjà vu), a smell, a peculiar abdominal sensation, fear or vertigo followed by an alteration of awareness, perhaps together with some automatic behaviour. The periods of vacancy tend to be longer than in petit mal and total awareness returns more slowly. Associated behavioural problems are common and at times it is difficult to decide which is a behavioural problem and which is an epileptic phenomenon. From the aura, some patients rapidly go into a tonic-clonic seizure. Sometimes temporal lobe attacks may present as rage episodes and very rarely as nightmares.

Skull radiographs may sometimes demonstrate an unequal size of the middle part of the skull due to atrophy or shrivelling of a temporal lobe. An EEG is helpful in distinguishing between petit mal and temporal lobe epilepsy, especially if the patient is drowsy or asleep at the time it is recorded.

More recent studies that have been carried out in both children and adults suggest that seizures that may be characterised principally by cessation of awareness and activity, are more likely to originate from discharges in the temporal lobe than anywhere else. Additionally, it is also recognised that many persons who have tonic-clonic seizures have this as a result of epileptic discharge which originates in the temporal lobe but then spreads to the rest of the brain.

Myoclonic epilepsies of childhood: The myoclonic epilepsies may be either primary or secondary to some other underlying brain abnormality. They may occur in many differing forms and combinations. The following may occur together or separately – atonic-akinetic (drop attacks), head nods, atypical absences and automatisms, frank myoclonic phenomena (jerks of muscles or parts of the body), tonic-clonic seizures and minor status epilepticus (see below). Because of the similarity that some people's attacks may have to petit mal epilepsy they are sometimes referred to as having 'petit mal variant'.

With myoclonic epilepsy there is not the same response to overbreathing as there is with petit mal epilepsy or with some patients with temporal lobe epilepsy, and the EEG shows a slow and irregular spike and wave pattern. Attacks may be more common on waking (as with infantile spasms).

There is in some a strong association between intellectual impairment and the myoclonic epilepsies. The term *Lennox-Gastaut* syndrome has sometimes been applied to children who may have the combination of complex myoclonic epilepsy and intellectual impairment.

Myoclonic epilepsy may be seen in a number of neuro-degenerative disorders, such as the various forms of *Batten's disease*, and the slow virus infection known as sub-acute sclerosing panencephalitis. A progressive familial myoclonic epilepsy occurs in which amyloid bodies (Lafora bodies) are found on biopsy of the brain. This familial progressive myoclonic epilepsy is also sometimes known as *Unverricht's myoclonic epilepsy* and, as well as being associated with other seizure disorders, is usually also accompanied by a progressive dementia.

Even without a neurodegenerative disorder the developmental outlook and ultimate control of seizures is poor for many children with myoclonic epilepsy.

Focal epilepsy: This may be either sensory or motor with the seizures confined to one part of the body, and often with consciousness retained. The term *Jacksonian epilepsy* may be used. Focal attacks may progress and spread, and end in a full tonic-clonic seizure. A focal weakness and paralysis for a variable length of time may develop following a focal seizure and this is known as *Todd's paralysis*.

In adults, focal epilepsy essentially implies a localised anatomical epileptogenic lesion such as a scar or tumour. Although this form of seizure is quite common in hemiplegic children (e.g. cerebral palsy) a focal lesion is less commonly found in young children than it is in adults.

Epilepsia partialis continua is a continuous focal epilepsy often without loss of consciousness, but with appropriate focal weakness. A localised cerebral disorder may be causative or rarely a degenerative disorder. Response to medical treatment is often poor.

Reflex epilepsy: There are several reflex epilepsies, the most common being the so-called *photosensitive epilepsy* or 'television epilepsy'. Seizures may be induced by being close to the television in some, when the 'hold' is not correctly adjusted. Discotheques can pose similar problems. The photic stimulation given during the routine EEG may identify spike discharges at certain flicker rates. In some people there may seemingly be an uncontrollable 'pull' towards the flickering television. Seizures or EEG spikes may be induced by just waving the fingers in front of the eyes while looking towards bright light. Treatment with many anticonvulsants is unhelpful.

Prolonged seizures (status epilepticus): This is a series of tonic-clonic seizures without intervening recovery of consciousness, and is a medical emergency. Prolonged and continuous seizure activity will cause cerebral oedema (brain swelling), hypoxia (lack of oxygen), hyperpyrexia (very high temperature) and death. Frequent prolonged seizures will cause brain scarring. While a specific aetiology may not be apparent, it is recognised that sudden withdrawal of anticonvulsant medication can be a cause of status epilepticus. An encephalitis may start with status epilepticus.

Minor motor status epilepticus is a form of status epilepticus where there is continuous minor motor seizure activity; the clinical picture may include marked mental dulling, drooling, with perhaps small jerks or twitches of the limbs or the face. At times, minor motor status epilepticus will herald the onset of a progressive cerebral disease. Prompt medical treatment will fortunately often return a child to near normality. The EEG is a helpful investigation as it will confirm seizure activity.

Adults

In general the most common inception times for seizures are during childhood and adolescent years. As already mentioned, in intellectually impaired populations seizures tend to be of an even earlier onset than they are in the remainder of the population. Nevertheless, seizures may occur first in adulthood and in later life, due in some to the normal ageing process but in others specific brain changes that are part of their primary condition, e.g. Alzheimer's disease in Down's syndrome.

THE MANAGEMENT OF EPILEPSY

Principles of drug therapy

The principle management of a person with recurrent seizures is most usually the employment of an anticonvulsant drug. For most this means commitment to such therapy for a significant length of time and care is, therefore, needed in deciding who requires such treatment. There seems to be little to justify the institution of anticonvulsant therapy when the person has had only a single seizure – indeed the same can be said for a person who has had two seizures. If it is decided that medication is required then it is important at all times to have a clear idea of what the aims of such treatment are to be. These should be, in the ideal situation, to prevent further seizures occurring or, failing this, that the seizures will be less frequent and less severe. At the same time it is vital to recognise that medication can severely compromise a person's ability to learn and cope with daily activities. The adverse affect of anticonvulsants is not always related to the amount that is being given.

The facility to measure levels of anticonvulsants and drugs in the blood has rendered therapy more rational and perhaps more scientific. Interaction between different drugs has been realised and with this the realisation that therapy should always commence with one drug. Interactions that may occur can be due either to the stimulation of enzyme activity so the level of another drug in the body is decreased or the inhibition of enzyme systems which means that the level of another drug will be increased.

Phenobarbitone: This is the most well known and certainly the oldest anticonvulsant drug still being employed. It has potent anticonvulsant activity and can be effective in a number of seizure disorders in adults and children, with the exception of infantile spasms, petit mal epilepsy, myoclonic epilepsy and the photosensitive epilepsies. It is the drug of choice in the neonate and has been advocated by many in the prevention of seizures due to fever in young children. But in a high proportion of children there are known side-effects with phenobarbitone, including learning disorders and behavioural disorders. It is for this reason that many paediatricians are reluctant to employ the drug.

Phenytoin: This first-line anticonvulsant has a proven ability in a number of differing seizure disorders, both in childhood and in adulthood. It is not an easy drug to use because blood levels are not easily predictable from the doses given.

There are several side-effects listed, perhaps the most well known is due to acute toxicity. These include ataxia (unsteadiness), dysarthria (indistinct speech) and extreme mental dulling, together with a deterioration in seizure control. The more chronic side-effects include gum hypertrophy (swelling), hirsuitism (hairiness), and thickening of subcutaneous tissue of cosmetic significance. A variety of blood problems and bone disease are also listed among the chronic side-effects.

It is important to recognise that this drug may have a significant effect on behaviour and learning ability in school and a particularly adverse affect on concentration. The effects may be so insidious as to be recognisable only retrospectively when the drug is removed.

Carbamazepine: This is a highly effective anticonvulsant in tonic-clonic seizures and partial seizures with either simple (focal epilepsy) or complex symptomatology (psychomotor or temporal lobe epilepsy).

Although a number of side-effects are listed in conjunction with this drug including skin rashes and initial drowsiness and apathy it is relatively free of side-effects compared to some other drugs. Therapy has always to be commenced slowly to reduce the risk of drowsiness.

Benzodiazepines. All of the benzodiazepines have, to varying extents, anticonvulsant, together with hypnotic and anxiolytic properties.

Diazepam is used widely in the treatment of prolonged seizures and status epilepticus, but is less effective in the long-term management of patients with seizures as tolerance (getting used to the drug) rapidly seems to develop.

Nitrazepam may be used for the treatment of myoclonic epilepsy whether this manifests as infantile spasms or myoclonic epilepsy of later childhood or adolescence. Sedative side-effects may restrict its use, although tolerance in this respect may be quite considerable.

Clonazepam was the first of the benzodiazepines specifically developed as an anticonvulsant. It is said to have a longer half-life than the other benzodiazepines and a lesser tendency to develop tolerance. Behavioural side-effects of this drug are common and personal experience suggests that tolerance, in spite of claims made to the contrary, sometimes develops.

Ethosuximide: Many feel that this remains the drug of first choice in the treatment of patients with true petit mal epilepsy. It may have gastrointestinal side-effects particularly when administration is only once daily but on the whole it is a drug that is relatively free of such problems.

Sodium valproate: This is the newest of the major anticonvulsants and is effective in several different seizure types – tonic-clonic seizures, myoclonic seizures, photosensitive epilepsy, and petit mal absences. It is perhaps less effective in the treatment of partial seizures.

Compared to most other anticonvulsants it is relatively free of side-effects although some do exist. Most commonly these are gastrointestinal and feature particularly when the drug is first introduced. This problem can be overcome by administration on a full stomach. Transitory alopecia (loss of hair) may occur in a small proportion of people; this is a reversible phenomenon.

Concerns have existed over damage to the liver, although to date well documented cases of serious liver disease as a consequence of this drug alone are very few in number.

Rectal administration

Whatever anticonvulsant drug is employed it is not possible to get away from the occurrence of side-effects of one sort or another in some persons. For this reason interest has centred in more recent times around the intermittent use of anticonvulsants. Administration of drugs such as diazepam rectally with a rapid absorption by that route has been of value in the management of a number of recurrent seizures in children that occur in spite of maintenance anticonvulsant therapy; particularly in those who have a tendency towards prolonged seizures.

Steroid medication

Steroid medication has a beneficial effect in some patients in whom anticonvulsants have not been adequately controlling attacks. These may particularly be used in the treatment of minor status epilepticus (see above).

Withdrawal and alteration of medication

Once it has been decided that a person needs anticonvulsant medication it is anticipated that this will be continued for at least two years following the last seizure. Withdrawal, however, should not take place at the time of puberty in the case of a child and should always be gradual over some weeks or months.

If there is thought to be a need to change from one drug to another this should be done by a gradual introduction of the new drug and an attempted gradual withdrawal of the previous drug.

Ketogenic diet

The so-called ketogenic diet has been employed for many years although interest in this method of treatment for epilepsy has been re-kindled in more recent times. There are two principal forms of the diet. The 'classical' diet is one in which a high fat content is provided by means of cream, the fats being in a ratio to carbohydrate of 4 to 1. An alternative has been the MCT diet in which the fat content is given by means of mixing in MCT oil (medium chain triglycerides) with a number of the foods taken.

Surgery for epilepsy

The surgical treatment of epilepsy has attracted significant literature and it would appear that there are indications for this form of management in some persons in whom medical management alone has been unsatisfactory. The commonest surgical treatment in epilepsy is temporal lobectomy – the removal of a temporal lobe of the brain. The generally accepted criteria for this particular operation are (1) that there has first been resistance to all drug therapy, (2) the persons are of reasonable intelligence with no evidence of a large tumour, and (3) the EEG focus is predominantly on one side. A more recent surgical development has been the employment of cerebellar stimulation through an implanted electrode. So far the results of this type of management have been equivocal and it remains to be seen as to whether this holds out hope for those in whom nothing else seems to have been successful.

SOCIAL AND EMOTIONAL PHENOMENA

In the total management of people with a seizure disorder there is a crucial need for there to be an open interaction and communication between the doctor, the patient, the parents of a child patient, educational and care staff. Time has to be given to discuss the nature of the problem the person has, the rationale of treatment and the specific problems that might be anticipated. Many of the problems that beset children and adults with epilepsy will be aggravated by undue restriction of activities. Nevertheless, it has to be recognised that there are risks in relation to activities such as swimming, crossing roads, operating machinery and a number of other activities.

Hyperkinetic behavioural problems recognised in a number of children have a fairly close association with some of the seizure disorders. However, medication may account for this behavioural pattern in a large proportion, particularly phenobarbitone and primidone. The newer drug, clonazepam, may have similar behavioural effects. However, the causes of hyperkinesis in a child with a seizure disorder must be recognised as multifactorial as is the case in similar children without seizures.

Specific behavioural problems may include so-called rage outbursts. Occasionally this may be seen with temporal lobe epilepsy, particularly when the problem is long-standing and originates in early life. The very complexity of temporal lobe discharges and their effects upon psychological function has been of specific interest to many. The knowledge that persons with a left temporal lobe lesion may have a definite psychopathic behaviour to a greater extent than those with right-sided lesions increases interest within this area.

It has already been emphasised that epilepsy is a common problem in intellectually impaired persons. The problems that this may cause are well-known to the families of intellectually impaired persons and their carers. But in spite of the frequency of epilepsy in this section of the population mistaken diagnosis and sub-optimal treatment is common. Many are labelled as having epilepsy when they do not have it, those who have complex absences are automatically referred to as having petit mal epilepsy, medication that is given is often wholly inappropriate or inadequate and the lives of persons with epilepsy may be unduly restricted and confined.

It is essential that if epilepsy is to be diagnosed correctly and treated, greater care needs to be taken on the part of not only medical but all care staff.

CEREBRAL PALSY

Cerebral palsy is the name that is applied to a group of disorders that share in common a physical defect due to some form of damage that occurs to the young and developing brain. It will manifest in a number of different ways and these differing manifestations will be discussed.

The physical defects that occur in cerebral palsy vary greatly in severity but always, in one way or another, affect what is referred to as 'motor function'. The cerebral palsies are a group of motor disorders due to something that damages the brain either before birth, during birth or within the early years of life. Although the nature of the motor disorders will vary as the child gets older, the damage that has occurred is not progressive.

WHAT IS KNOWN ABOUT CAUSATION?

In a proportion of children with cerebral palsy, about 30 per cent, the cause is not known. In those where it is known nearly 75 per cent are due to something that has occurred before birth (pre-natally) or at the time of birth (peri-natally); the remainder occur after birth (post-natally).

Pre-natal causes

The number of possible or probable causes is very large. In a very small proportion of the less common varieties of cerebral palsy there may be a genetic basis. An infection that passes from the mother to the fetus *may* mean that the infant has cerebral palsy. Prominent among such infections may be a virus known as cytomegalovirus, an infestation called toxoplasmosis, the viral infection rubella (German measles) or the virus infection herpes simplex (the last tends to be something that occurs very late in pregnancy – often during the actual birth). Miscarriages or abortions *may* be associated with the ultimate development of cerebral palsy or any other event that jeopardises the functions of the placenta. Various factors may predispose the fetus to being damaged such as maternal disease of many sorts.

Peri-natal causes

There are several things that may go wrong in relation to the birth of a baby; fortunately for most these do not cause lasting problems. But in some they do. If the baby is born prematurely problems may result as a consequence. The baby is immature in many ways. The lungs may be immature and with this there will be breathing problems and the brain may not get enough oxygen – this is called asphyxia or sometimes hypoxia. The brain itself is immature and bleeds readily into either the cavities of the brain – the ventricles – or into the substance of the brain itself. Infections are difficult to combat. All these problems are particularly common in the very small baby under 1500g – who previously seldom survived at all. In some situations there may be a rapid breakdown of the baby's blood cells, either because there is interaction between the blood cells of the baby and the mother or because of particular abnormalities of the blood cells themselves or in the presence of severe infection. Because the liver is still immature, even in the full-term baby, broken-down red cells accumulate and jaundice occurs. If this is severe it can damage the brain – some parts more than others – and give rise to a condition called kernicterus, which later produces a form of cerebral palsy known as dyskinetic cerebral palsy.

Post-natal causes

Any number of events may damage the young brain after birth, and in such a way as to cause cerebral palsy. Infections of the brain – meningitis or encephalitis – can cause a variety of lasting problems, including cerebral palsy. Injuries to the brain may cause cerebral palsy. In some infants a stroke may occur. Finally, it is important to say that in any number of serious generalised illnesses the baby may be left with cerebral palsy.

HOW COMMON IS CEREBRAL PALSY

It is difficult in any population to estimate what is the true incidence of cerebral palsy. In those who are only mildly affected the diagnosis may not be made until the child is 6 or much later. One of the most reliable estimates in Britain is from research work co-ordinated from Bristol – the estimate is approximately 2.4:1000 births (personal communication). It is, however, important to recognise that estimates even in highly developed countries may be very unreliable and certainly appear to vary markedly from one area or centre to another.

WHAT FORMS OF CEREBRAL PALSY ARE THERE?

The commonest forms of cerebral palsy are the so-called spastic types, hence the 'nickname' for children and adults with cerebral palsy of 'spastics'. Spasticity is a medical term that is applied to a particular form of stiffness that affects muscles and indicates that the primary abnormality is in a particular part of the brain responsible for the movement of muscles and parts of the body.

There are several varieties of spastic cerebral palsy: *hemiplegia* which affects one side of the body (the arm to a greater extent than the leg); *diplegia* which affects both legs; and *quadriplegia* which affects all four limbs. The other varieties of cerebral palsy have different motor abnormalities. In the dyskinetic cerebral palsies the main problem is with uncontrolled or involuntary movements which vary in both severity and character. There are three varieties: *athetosis* which is a slow, sometimes writhing movement most obvious in small muscles such as the hands; *chorea* which is a more rapid jerky movement, more marked in the large muscles such as the shoulders; and *dystonia* which is an abnormality that produces sudden stiffening movements and postures that may affect a part of even almost the whole body when it is severe. It can affect mobility, speech and many aspects of daily activities. Other non-specific forms of cerebral palsy include 'ataxic' cerebral palsy in which floppiness of the muscles persists, and significant general unsteadiness. Also included in the non-spastic forms of cerebral palsy will be 'hypotonic' cerebral palsy in which the main feature is that the infant and child are very floppy and double jointed.

There are two important points in relation to the physical features of the cerebral palsies.

The first point is that the picture we see in the older infant and child may not have existed in that child when in early infancy. The very spastic child initially may have been very floppy, the dyskinetic child may also have been floppy, only later developing the involuntary movements that characterise this particular sub-group. The picture in many will change as the child gets older and the brain matures.

The second point is that no matter what the textbooks say, there is very often an overlap between the different varieties of cerebral palsy. In the hemiplegic child there will often be some involvement of the 'good' side and in the affected hand there may be some athetoid posturings. In the diplegic child there will often be some problems with the hands. Every child needs individual careful evaluation, a 'label' is not enough.

OTHER NON-MOTOR PROBLEMS

Emphasis has thus far been on the motor or physical aspects of cerebral palsy. There are other problems that *may* occur in children and adults with this group of conditions. Many, but by no means all, children will have learning difficulties. In some these will be severe, in others mild and very specific. In general the more severe the cerebral palsy in physical terms, the more severe will be the learning difficulties, but this relationship is by no means fixed.

About 30 per cent of children and adults with cerebral palsy (mostly those with a hemiplegia or quadriplegia) will have epilepsy. In some it is the epilepsy that may be the major problem.

Hearing problems are very common, most of all with dyskinetic cerebral palsy. Visual problems of various sorts are common – in over 40 per cent of children with cerebral palsy.

Speech and language difficulties occur – particularly in those who have a severe form of cerebral palsy.

Not least are emotional problems. They may be significant in the older cerebral palsied child and adult as they experience greater difficulty in fully integrating into their peer group.

CAN CEREBRAL PALSY BE PREVENTED?

It would seem fitting to ask this question. In Europe the incidence of dyskinetic cerebral palsy has dramatically dropped. This is due to the commonest form of blood group incompatibility between mother and fetus – Rhesus disease – being effectively prevented.

Undoubtedly a greater number of babies who in previous years were born with cerebral palsy are now born without. This difference or change is due in no small measure to a greater understanding of the management and monitoring of labour and delivery and equally a greater understanding of the care of the sick newborn – particularly the premature newborn. All of this requires not only dedicated professional staff, but well trained dedicated staff working in premises that have the essential equipment to provide a high level of care.

It is perhaps important at least to touch upon the problems of what we refer to as the very-low-birth-weight baby. A decade ago, certainly two decades ago, these very small babies (under 1500g) did not survive; many now do. But do they survive with or without a deficit? No one really knows the answer to that question. Careful follow-up studies are being conducted in several centres in Britain and elsewhere and it is hoped that some answers may be found when the results are known.

It has been argued for many years that following the diagnosis of cerebral palsy in a child, comprehensive and multiprofessional assessment of strengths and weaknesses should be undertaken. But it is generally agreed that assessment is not a specific activity undertaken at one point in time, but an activity that should be continuous. While the association between cerebral palsy and learning difficulties is well described, particular care is needed in the assessment of children with severe communication problems because all too often such children are automatically assumed to be severely intellectually impaired. Care has to be taken to ensure that a specific sensory impairment, such as a hearing loss, is recognised.

In those people with cerebral palsy and significant mobility problems, the physical limitations that exist for them are inevitably going to impair some aspects of their social and cognitive development. While this may produce inaccurate assessments of their intellectual ability in early childhood, in later childhood and adolescence their motivation both physically and emotionally may be impaired.

FURTHER ASSOCIATED POINTS

This chapter has discussed in detail two of the most common and important associated medical conditions in people with severe intellectual impairment. It would be as wrong as it would be incomplete to suggest that the story ended with the discussion of these two groups of conditions. There is a whole multitude of medical conditions that exist with far greater frequency in those with severe intellectual impairment than exist in other members of society.

Disorders of the special senses are particularly common. Severe and varied visual problems are common in people with Down's syndrome (in nearly half) and in those with severe cerebral palsy. Cataracts, as well as abnormalities at the back of eye, are a feature of those whose brain damage is as a result of a congenital infection – rubella, toxoplasmosis and cytomegalovirus. But besides these specific associations, problems with vision are much more common in all with severe intellectual impairments.

Hearing problems are more common, children with Down's syndrome being particularly vulnerable, and in adults with Down's syndrome progressive nerve deafness is well described. Again, it is important to be certain that hearing is normal in any severely intellectually impaired person, as failure to recognise even a mild to moderate loss can have a significantly adverse effect on that person's development.

In more recent years attention has focused on two areas of concern in people with Down's syndrome. Abnormalities of the thyroid gland – most commonly an underactivity – become more common with age. Recognition of underactivity when it exists is important, for giving of thyroid supplements can have a very beneficial effect upon general and specific well-being.

The second area of concern has been over instability between the base of the skull and the top of the neck. The exact significance of this well recognised instability has yet to be finally quantified, but in the present state of knowledge certain contact activities – trampolining and diving head first into swimming pools – are probably contra-indicated because of the danger of damaging the spinal cord.

Besides these specific medical associations it should be recognised that a wide range of medical problems occurs with greater frequency and presents more difficulties in diagnosis than in other people. In the multiply handicapped person chest infections can go unrecognised until the individual is desperately ill. Even specific surgical conditions such as appendicitis are diagnosed later than they otherwise might be. Dental health is often neglected and acute dental problems not recognised for what they are.

There is much to suggest that the basic medical care given to people with severe intellectual impairment is not of the same standard as for other members of society. It is argued that this group of people overall has a greater need for good medical care than the rest of society.

Epilogue
Future Changes

In the field of mental handicap, changes have started in the UK which were almost unthinkable 12 years ago. The recent realisation that people with severe learning difficulties are themselves capable of major growth and development is a change of enormous significance. While this book has emphasised positive change, there are world events leading to some likely changes for the worse, and an effort must be made to anticipate them. It is also especially important to identify those areas of change in which recent progress remains vulnerable, in order to maintain the vigilance and effort necessary to secure those achievements.

POPULATION

In Western countries there has been a significant reduction in the numbers of children with severe learning difficulties. While birth rates have fallen, the tremendous efforts made through genetic counselling, improved obstetrics, child health developments and health education programmes to prevent the occurrence of impairments are all bearing fruit. Although medical technology is enabling the survival of very premature babies who once would certainly have died, 1 in 8 of them is likely to have major disabilities. In developing countries widespread influences (both positive and negative) are having their impacts on whole new generations. In India for example, the national Integrated Child Development Project has aimed to deliver obstetric, nutritional, immunisation and health education to all mothers and young children for almost a decade. As a result of this exciting project the overall health of the new generation of growing children is much improved, but within it are those children now surviving with major disabilities to face a highly uncertain future as adults. (It must be said that even rich countries providing early childhood interventions never seem to recognise that adulthood with its new needs is only 15 years or less ahead.) We know that chronic, severe malnutrition of pregnant women permanently restricts brain development in the children they carry. It is an appalling fact that *one-sixth of the world's population* is affected, so that whole societies may be left intellectually disabled as a result.

The world-wide pandemic of AIDS has already reached a small number of children born to infected mothers, and others have been infected from blood products needed in the treatment of their haemophilia. There is as yet limited experience of the illness in children, but we know that the infecting organism (human immuno virus (HIV)) can invade and destroy brain cells. It can be expected that increasing numbers of children will be brain damaged by this means before a protective vaccine or treatment are available.

SOCIAL STATUS

The changes in social status may be seen by some as the most fundamental of all. They are patchy, slow and vulnerable: they will demand the utmost tenacity in the face of organisational and political indifference, complacency or actual opposition. The affirmation of people with severe learning difficulties as having equal human value with every one else, together with the fresh design and delivery of the kind of services *they* prefer and which enhance their image, turn traditional attitudes and provisions upside down. Changing their own social status requires the active support of people with a mental handicap through learning to be assertive about their own interests and choices. For some individuals or political groups the lifting of people they have always perceived as the bottom of the human ladder, to levels of equity, so shatters their sense of hierarchy and their own place in it, as to be unthinkable and intolerable. Although the growing autonomy and confidence of individuals with severe learning difficulties is a source of joy to their friends, it can be disturbing to others who have deep, confused fears about disabilities and being 'different', and they may resist consciously or unconsciously all serious efforts to ensure the status of equal citizenship. In times of economic and emotional stress, the capacity for social tolerance usually contracts, and old prejudices and priorities surface. In the UK the political status of people with intellectual disabilities has improved slightly: some hospital residents have actually regained voting rights, but the situation remains fragile. Their problems are not vote catching, and it must be asked how politically interesting are those people who will always need much support, in an economic and political climate which adulates those 'who can stand on their own feet'. An Indian saying reminds us that if you worship success, you guarantee inadequacy. The social and political status of people with severe learning difficulties will always be vulnerable in a society based on winners and losers; their rights must be watched vigilantly and promoted by every means possible, by all people of goodwill.

TECHNIQUES AND TECHNOLOGY

Enormous strides have been made in both education and therapy, with improvements in methods of teaching, and in awareness of the crucial role of the environment in facilitating or hindering learning. We know that congregated, segregated activities do not support personal development as effectively as individualised ones. This applies especially to those people whose behaviour presents problems. There is a variety of techniques which would be very valuable to many with a mental handicap if they were taught to use them regularly, including relaxation methods and alternative methods of communication. Physical aids, in particular electronic developments, can help with sensory, communication and mobility disabilities: however, they are available to only a very tiny number of the people who need them. One of the reasons why techniques and technology are not being applied is that dissemination of new knowledge has a poor standing in the statutory services.

In-service training has such low priority that research findings take years to reach service deliverers, and often become distorted and diluted in the process anyway. It can safely be said that before we demand *more* research the lives of people with a mental handicap could be transformed, simply by widely applying the knowledge that research has already provided. If carers are to acquire the new techniques and technology, and in turn incorporate them regularly in the lives of the people who need them (but who are currently denied them) then there must be the political will to give the task priority, and the funding to carry it out.

CARE IN THE COMMUNITY AND FINANCE

'Care in the community' is now a thoroughly devalued term: many of its opponents misunderstand the model, and assert that 'care *by* the community' will not work, as the community is uncaring. The movement arose from the ideological concern that people should have the necessary services delivered to them in their own local community in the least restrictive environment. In the early days many people with only *mild* disabilities left hospital successfully, and used ordinary existing community resources for many of their needs. The costs of their community supports were lower than average hospital costs. The UK government's original financial promotion of the resettlement of hospital residents in local communities hinted wistfully that 'care in the community' might be cheaper than institutional care: that illusion was rapidly dispelled. Care delivered in the community requires more investment, not less, than that in the hospitals. The vast majority of people with grave disabilities are looked after at home by relatives, often single handed. British society pays them an attendance allowance of £1612 per annum for providing the 24-hour care. Full residential care in a home run by a voluntary organisation costs around £25,000, and NHS hospitals spend an average of £12,000 on each of their residents. That sum of £12,000 can be transferred with hospital residents who are resettled in the community, but no such money has been allocated to serve the severely disabled individuals at home totally dependent on ageing relatives. There are not even places available in the hospitals now, because the transfer of financial resources with residents moving out, means that the vacated places must be closed down.

Care in the community needs adequate funding, planned over several years. The present system whereby statutory agencies do not know their budgets for more than a year or two at a time encourages inefficient, haphazard developments. Without realistic funding, community projects will be started without sufficient background knowledge or staff training and support. Resultant failures will be welcomed by those who do not want change, and the unsung successes and lessons will be ignored in the ensuing public outcry.

Shortage of money is equally disastrous as an argument with which to promote institutional rather than community care. There is no way in which hospitals can continue on the present financial basis. They are mostly old, decaying and appallingly expensive to heat, repair and maintain. More money will need to be found, whatever the model of service.

Bibliography

Craft, M., Bicknell, J. and Hollins, S. (eds.) (1985). *Mental Handicap: A Multidisciplinary Approach*. Baillière Tindall, London.

Office of Health Economics/MENCAP (1986). *Mental Handicap: Partnership in the Community*. HMSO, London.

Russell, O. (1985). *Mental Handicap*. Churchill Livingstone, Edinburgh.

King's Fund Centre (1980). *An Ordinary Life*. Project Paper No. 24. King's Fund, London.

Useful Addresses

UNITED KINGDOM

Advocacy Alliance
  c/o One-to-One, 16 Chenies Street
  London WC1E 7ET

Association of Professions for the Mentally Handicapped (APMH)
  126 Albert Street
  London NW1 7NF

British Epilepsy Association
  Crowthorne House, Bigshotte
  New Wokingham Road, Wokingham RG11 3AW

British Institute of Mental Handicap
  Wolverhampton Road
  Kidderminster, Worcs DY10 3PP

British Sports Association for the Disabled
  Ludwig Guttmann House, Harvey Road
  Stoke Mandeville, Aylesbury Bucks HP21 8PP

Family Planning Association
  22 Sussex Place
  London NW1 4RG

Handicapped Adventure Playground Association
   Fulham Palace Playground, Bishops Avenue
   London SW6 6EE

Invalid Children's Aid Association
   126 Buckingham Palace Road
   London SW1 9SB

For all handicaps and with a special interest in language disorders

National Association for Mental Health (MIND)
   22 Harley Street
   London W1N 3ED

National Society for Autistic Children
   276 Willesden Lane
   London NW2 5RB

Royal Society for the Mentally Handicapped Child and Adult
   (MENCAP)
   123 Golden Lane
   London EC1 0RT

Spastics Society
   12 Park Crescent
   London W1N 4EQ

Voluntary Council for Handicapped Children
   The National Children's Bureau
   8 Wakley Street, London EC1V 7QE

INTERNATIONAL

Commonwealth Association for Mental Handicap and
   Developmental Disabilities
   c/o 36a Osberton Place
   Sheffield S11 8XL

Cerebral Palsy Overseas
   6 Duke's Mews
   London W1M 5RB

International League of Societies for Persons with
   Mental Handicap (ILSMH)
   13 rue Forestière
   B–1050, Brussels, Belgium

USA

The Centre on Human Policy
   123 College Place, Syracuse University
   Syracuse, NY 13244

The Association for Persons with Severe Handicaps (TASH)
   7010 Roosevelt Way
   Seattle WA 98115

CANADA

The Canadian Association for Community Living *and* the National
   Institute for Mental Retardation
   York University Campus
   4700 Keele Street, Downsview, Ontario M3J 1P3

Index

Acetylcholine, deficiency of, 190
Acrocephalosyndactyly, 200
Acts of Parliament, 134
Adenoma sebaceum, 202
Adolescence, problems of, 41
Adult Education, 97
Adult Training Centre (ATC), 7, 40,
    42, 82–6, 88, 159, 185
    physiotherapy in, 59
Adventure holidays, 96
Age of consent, 134
Ageing process, 179
Aggression, 165
AIDS, cause of brain damage in
    children, 235
Alzheimer's disease, 188–91
Amniocentesis, 208
Anti-social behaviour, 87
Anticonvulsants, 219–23
Anxiety, 166
Apert's Syndrome, 200
Arteriosclerosis, 188–91
Attendance Allowance, 11, 238
Autism, 17

Ball games, value of, 93
Behaviour modification, 169–70
Benzodiazepines, 221–2
'Better Services for the Mentally
    Handicapped', 26–7
Biochemical disorders as cause of
    mental handicap, 207–8
Biochemical impairments, 153
Birth of handicapped child, response
    to, 33–7
Blindness, 157
Bloch-Sulzberger disease, 200
Bournville's disease, 202
Brain damage, 153

Brain swelling, 219
Burn-out among carers in mental
    handicap, 142–50

Camping, 95–6
Carbamazepine, 221
Catholic Church, attitude to mental
    handicap, 23
Central nervous system:
    disorders of, 198–204
    infection of, 208
Cerebral gigantism, 201–2
Cerebral oedema, 219
Cerebral palsy, 8, 10–12, 154–6,
    226–31
    causes of, 226–8
    prevention of, 230–1
Charitable organisations, 81
Child psychiatry, 14–15
Choice-making, 135
Chorea, 229
Chromosomal causes of mental
    handicap, 197–8
Classification of mental handicap,
    2–4, 25
Clonazepam, 222, 225
Collecting, value of to individual, 94
Colleges of Further Education, 75–6
Communication, 155–6
    aids for, 62
Community care, 5–6, 26, 104, 237–8
    intr   tion of, 120–2
Computer aided communication, 62
Computerised axial tomography
    (CT scan), 213
Conditioning, 170
Conflict among support staff, 147–8
Consensus decision-making, 49–51
Contraception, 131

Control, exertion of, 46–7
Coordinator, role of in assessment, 52–3
Cost of care, 5
Council of Europe, 67, 69
Curricula, in special schools, 71
Cytomegalovirus (CMV), 205, 232

Dancing, 95
Darwin, Charles, 24
Deafness, 86, 157
Decision-taking by mentally
    handicapped people, 84–5
Dementia, 188–91
Denmark, services in, 27
Depression, 166
Derbyshire Local Education Authority,
    74
Description, process of, 45
Diazepam, 221
Diet, ketogenic, 223
Diet modification, 167
Disruptive behaviour, 87
Divorce, 135
Down's Syndrome, 7–8, 92, 154, 184–
    5, 189, 191, 232
    premature ageing in, 187
Drug administration, rectal, 222–3
Drug therapy:
    for behaviour control, 167
    for epilepsy, 219–23
Drugs, as cause of mental handicap, 204

Education, 39
    adult 97
Education Act (1970), 27
Education Act (1981), 73–4
Electroencephalography, 211, 213
Electronically-aided communication, 62
Emotional changes in old age, 180–2
Employment Rehabilitation Centres
    (ERCs), 81
Encephalitis, 208
Environmental aspects of care, 168
Epilepsia partialis continua, 218
Epilepsy, 86, 91, 167, 211–25
    classification of, 212
    diagnosis of, 212
    management of, 219–25
Epiloia, 202
Eternal child model, 124, 128
Ethosuximide, 222
Eugenics movement, 125
Evolution, theory of, 24
Explanation, understanding by, 46

Familial dysautonomia, 201
Family, dynamics of, 32–3
Family Planning Association, 131
Feeding difficulties, 38
Fetal Alcohol Syndrome, 204
Fishing, 94
Focal epilepsy, 218
Foreign travel, benefit of, 96

Galactosaemia, 207
Gardening, rewards of, 95
Genetic causes of mental handicap,
    197–8
Genetics, 152–4
Goals, setting of, 51–2
Grandparents, role of, 36
Group homes, compatibility of
    occupants, 120–1
Guiding for handicapped people, 96

Head injuries, 208–9
Hearing problems in cerebral palsy, 230
Herpes simplex, 206
High-risk sports for handicapped
    people, 91–2
History of treatment in mental
    handicap, 20–2
Hobbies, choice of, 90–1, 93–5
Holidays, needs of handicapped people,
    95–6
Home, provision of, 106–11
Hydrocephalus, 198–9
Hyperpyrexia, 219
Hypocalcaemia, 207
Hypoglycaemia, 207, 212
Hypothyroidism, 190–1, 208
Hypoxia, 219

Incontinence, 86, 189
Incontinentia Pigmenti, 200
Independence, as measure of quality of
    life, 72
India, initiatives in, 235
Individuality, destruction of by
    institutionalisation, 115–17
Infantile spasms, 214–15
Institutionalisation, 112–19
Integrated Child Development Project,
    India, 235
Intellectual changes in old age, 180
Intelligence Quotient (IQ), 24–5, 66
Intervention, 174–5
Intra-uterine infections, 205–6

Jacksonian epilepsy, 218
Jay Committee, 27

Ketogenic diet, 223
Key-Worker:
  in assessment, 54
  role of, 106–7, 149–50

L-dopa deficiency, 190
Language:
  as environment control, 157–8
  use of, 61, 155–6
Laurence-Moon-Beidl Syndrome,
  199–200
Legislation, 26, 133–5
Leisure activities, choice of, 90–1
Lennox-Gastaut Syndrome, 217
Lesch-Nyhan Syndrome, 166
Life expectancy of mentally
  handicapped people, 184–7
Literacy, acquisition of, 60
Lobectomy, temporal, 224
Local Education Authorities,
  responsibility of, 73–4
Loneliness in old age, 181–2
Long-term care, 105–6, 109–11
Lunacy Act (1890), 126

Manpower Services Commission
  (MSC), 81–2
Marriage of mentally handicapped
  people, 131–2, 135
Masturbation, 18, 130
Maternal Phenylketonuria, 204–5
Memory loss, 188–9
MENCAP, 97
Mental Deficiency Acts (1912 and
  1913), 25, 66, 126
Mental handicap, society's view of,
  100–3
Mental Health Act (1959), 26–7
Mental Health Act (1983), 2
Mental illness, confusion with mental
  handicap, 29, 101
Microcephaly, 199
Migraine, 212
Minor motor status epilepticus, 219
Mourning, process of, 33–4
Multiple sclerosis, 155
Music, enjoyment of, 94
Myoclonic epilepsies of childhood,
  217–18

National Health Service, 4
  establishment of, 25

Neurocutaneous Syndromes, 202
Neurofribromatosis, 202–3
Nitrazepam, 221–2
Numeracy, acquisition of, 60

Occupational therapy, 59–61
Outward Bound courses for
  handicapped people, 91

Pain, as cause of disruptive behaviour,
  165–6
Parenthood among mentally
  handicapped people, 132
Parkinson's disease, 190
Paroxysmal vertigo, 212
Participation, as measure of quality of
  life, 72–3
Pavlov, Ivan, 170
Peri-natal causes of mental handicap,
  206–7
Peter Pan Syndrome, 192
Petit mal, 215–16
Phakomatoses, 202
Phenobarbitone, 220, 225
Phenothiazines, 101
Phenylketonuria (PKU), 153–4, 166,
  207–8
Phenytoin, 220–1
Physical problems of mentally
  handicapped people, 86–7
Physical restraint, 175
Physiotherapy, 57–9
Pilot Parents, 37
Predictability, 45–6
Premature ageing in Down's
  Syndrome, 8, 187
'Preparation for Life' Project of Council
  of Europe, 67–8
Primidone, 225
Productivity, as measure of quality of
  life, 72
Psychiatric illness, among mentally
  handicapped people, 158
Psychiatry, child, 14–15
Psychomotor epilepsy, 216–17
Punishment to produce acceptable
  behaviour, 173

Quality of life, evaluation of, 72–3

Recreational skills, development of, 90
Rectal administration of drugs, 222–3
Reflex epilepsy, 218
Relationships, 124

Religion and mental handicap, 23
Restraint, physical, 175
Rights of mentally handicapped people, 4–5
Riley-Day Syndrome, 201
Risk-taking in leisure activities, 91–2
Royal Commission on law relating to mental illness (1954), 26
Rubella, 206, 232

Scouting for handicapped people, 96
Security, developing feelings of, 171–2
Self-injurious behaviour, 165
Sex education, 19, 127–8
Sexual behaviour, 18
Sexual Offences Act (1956), 133–4
Sexuality, 7, 41, 125–6
    guidelines on, 132–3
    in old age, 181–2
    problems of, 123
    suppression of, 129–30
Short-term care:
    cost effectiveness of, 108
    provision of, 103–4
Sibling response to birth of handicapped child, 40
Signing, 62
Skull radiography, to diagnose epilepsy, 213
Sleep problems, 38
Smith-Lemli-Opitz Syndrome, 200–1
Social response to mental handicap, 22–31
Social skills, acquisition of, 60
Social status of mentally handicapped people, 235–6
Sodium valproate, 222
Sotos Syndrome, 201–2
Spasticity, 86, 228
Special schools, arguments for maintaining, 68–75
Speech therapy, 61–3
Spina bifida, 198–9
Sport, 90, 92
Staff:
    institutional, 117–19, 141–2
    quality of in care of handicapped people, 110–11
    reliability of, 172–3
Staff appraisal, 149
Status epilepticus, 218–19

Sterilisation of mentally handicapped people, 132
Steroid medication, 223
Stress among carers of mentally handicapped people, 142–50
Sturge-Weber Syndrome, 203–4
Support for parents of handicapped child, 36–9
Support services for mentally handicapped people, 137–51
Support staff:
    selection of, 138–9
    training of, 139–41
Surgery for epilepsy, 224
Sweden, services in, 27
Swimming, therapeutic value of, 92–3
Symbol-based communication, 62
Syncope, 212

Team spirit, 90
Teamwork as aid to assessment, 47
Temporal lobe epilepsy, 216–17
Temporal lobectomy, 224
Terminology of mental handicap, 2
Tetany, 212
Thyroid:
    abnormalities of, 232
    under-functioning of, 190–1
Todd's paralysis, 218
Tonic-clonic seizures, 215
TORCH infections, 205
Total institutions, 112–19
Toxoplasmosis, 205, 232
Tranquillisers, 101, 167
Tuberous Sclerosis, 202, 215

United States:
    employment of mentally handicapped people in, 87–8
    policy of 'deinstitutionalisation', 122
Unverricht's myoclonic epilepsy, 217

Visual problems in cerebral palsy, 230
Von Recklinghausen's disease, 203

Walking, value of, 94
Warnock Committee, 67
Warnock Report, 73
Work:
    importance of, 78–9
    purpose of in an institution, 114
World Health Organisation, 2